Charles Marsh Mead

Romans dissected:

A critical analysis of the Epistle to the Romans

Charles Marsh Mead

Romans dissected:
A critical analysis of the Epistle to the Romans

ISBN/EAN: 9783337729820

Printed in Europe, USA, Canada, Australia, Japan

Cover: Foto ©ninafisch / pixelio.de

More available books at **www.hansebooks.com**

ROMANS DISSECTED

A CRITICAL ANALYSIS OF THE

EPISTLE TO THE ROMANS

BY

E. D. M^cREALSHAM

EDINBURGH

T. & T. CLARK

NEW YORK

CHARLES SCRIBNER'S SONS

1891

CONTENTS.

CHAPTER I.
INTRODUCTORY REMARKS.

Sketch of previous attempts to analyse the Epistle. F. C. Baur. Weakness of his position. Bruno Bauer. C. H. Weisse. A. Pierson. A. D. Loman. R. Steck. Logical result of the Tübingen criticism. The fundamental assumptions of a sound criticism. These themselves practically make the genuineness of the Pauline Epistles inadmissible. But further proof required by some. The method here to be pursued. pp. 1—9.

CHAPTER II.
THE DOCTRINAL ARGUMENT.

A critical analysis of the Epistle discloses the work of four different authors, whom we call G^1, G^2, JC, and CJ. Characteristics of the several authors. (1) G^1 makes salvation depend on obedience to the law. He wrote i. 18—ii. 29, except ii. 16. Also xii. 9—xiii. 13. Reasons for this analysis. Finally, xvi. 17—20. Question about verse 18. Resemblance between G^1 and the Epistle of James. (2) G^2 makes salvation depend on faith in God. Begins at iii. 1. Contrast between him and G^1. Why iii. 21—26 must be assigned to JC. G^2 emphasises the divine sovereignty. The section iii. 27—iv. 24. Question about iv. 24.

Connection of this section with vii. 7—24, and of this with ix. 6—33, and ch. xi. — (3) JC makes faith in Christ's vicarious death the prominent thing. He wrote i. 1—17. Reasons for assigning ii. 16 to him. The sections iii. 21—26, iv. 25—v. 21, and ix. 1—5. Reasons for assigning ch. x. to JC. The final sections, xv. 8—13 and xvi. 21—27. (4) CJ. emphasises the doctrine that the Christian life is a life in the Spirit, union with Christ, and death to sin. Connection of vi. 2 *sqq*. with the foregoing. Difference between CJ and JC as to righteousness, justification, and faith. Ch. vi.—vii. 6 continued in ch. viii. The hortatory part, xii. 1—8, xiii. 14—xv. 7. The concluding section, xv. 14—33. Conclusion. pp. 10—39.

CHAPTER III.

THE LINGUISTIC ARGUMENT.

(1) The two forms "Jesus Christ" and "Christ Jesus". Coincidence of this difference with doctrinal differences. Possible reason for the diverse forms. (2) The ethical sense of σάρξ found only in CJ. Apparent exception. The corresponding sense of πνεῦμα. (3) Detailed linguistic analysis of the Epistle and comparison of the four writers. The result compared with a similar analysis of Gen. i.—xii, 5. Particular verbal differences in the four authors. Differences of style. — Völter's analysis of the Epistle. Comparison of the general result with that of Pentateuchal analysis. The question of chronological order in the latter. The critics' assumption of the genuineness of certain O. T. books. Probability that all are spurious. Objections answered.

pp. 40—71.

CHAPTER IV.

THE HISTORICAL ARGUMENT.

The alleged conflict between facts and theories. What are the historical arguments? The value of tradition. It must be subjected to criticism. The evidence respecting our Epistle. Our theory relieves us of many difficulties besetting the traditional view. (1) May not one of the four writers have been Paul? If any one, it must have been G^1. Reasons for a negative conclusion. (2) The allegations that there has never been any doubt of the Epistle's genuineness, and that it bears in itself and in its relation to the Acts evidences of being Pauline. Reply. Facility of ancient writers in producing and introducing forgeries. The indecisiveness of historical testimony. Probable date of the several parts of the Epistle. Epistle of Clement, etc. (3) Objection that forgeries could not so soon have got currency. Reply. Quotation from Steck. Ease of introducing pseudepigraphical writings. The objection, that it is improbable that no genuine writings of the early Christians are extant, answered.

pp. 72—93.

POSTSCRIPT.   pp. 94, 95.

CHAPTER I.

INTRODUCTORY REMARKS.

Since F. C. Baur's critique of the Pauline Epistles, the result of which was to leave only the first four of them as genuine, the most advanced criticism has for the most part been content to accept this conclusion as final, while some of Baur's followers have even beaten a retreat, and conceded the genuineness of more than these four Epistles. This timidity and wavering have proceeded from anything but a thoroughly critical spirit. Every intelligent man knows that the inspiring animus of this criticism was a conviction that Christianity must have been a gradual growth fully accounted for by the historical forces at work at the beginning of our era, and that the notion of supernatural agency must be ruled out. To concede that Paul really wrote the four principal Epistles bearing his name is, however, a concession which practically cuts the nerve of this whole critical system. It is a concession that Paul himself proclaimed supernaturalism

1

in its sharpest form; and the result is that these Epistles are assumed to date at the latest only 20 or 30 years from the time of Jesus, are admitted to be genuine, and (since Paul's honesty is not impugned) presumably authentic. Baur, to be sure, as an intelligent man, could not fully accept this conclusion, nor can his followers. Pfleiderer, for example, admires and eulogises Paul, but is unable to accept his theology, or even his testimony as to facts. Baur stood puzzled before the problem of Christ's resurrection, which the Pauline Epistles unequivocally affirm. He could not admit the fact of the resurrection: yet his respect for Paul made him afraid to be consistent enough to proclaim that Paul, in promulgating the story of Jesus' resurrection, was really promulgating a falsehood.

The traditionalists have not been slow to avail themselves of this weak point in the critical assault. They say, with force and plausibility, that this discrediting of the Gospels, the Acts, and the most of the Epistles is of little account, so long as these four Epistles are allowed to stand as presenting the substance of the Christianity which had all along been preached. The argument is strong: If the object is to overthrow supernaturalism, it can never be accomplished, so long as Paul's chief Epistles are conceded to be genuine. If they are genuine, then they represent not merely what Paul believed, but what the Christians of his time generally believed. He appeals to the universal belief of the Christian Church, when he affirms the reality of Christ's resurrection; and no one can consistently reject this doctrine without either impugning the trustworthiness of Paul or denying that Paul wrote the Epistles in question.

It is strange that the critics have been so shortsighted in their procedure. They have been so occupied with their halfway measure and with the defence of it against the assaults of their orthodox opponents, that they have failed to see that their only safety is neither in remaining where they are, nor in beating a retreat, but in boldly pushing forwards and assailing the strongholds which they have been trying to persuade themselves that they can safely leave in the hands of the enemy. Bruno Bauer[1], it is true, had the courage to deny the Pauline authorship of *all* the so-called Pauline Epistles; but his work was hardly noticed by either of the two main contending parties. He belonged to no party, and his work seemed to be killed by silence. For more than thirty years no one in Germany ventured to join him in his bold effort. C. H. Weisse[2], it is true, undertook to sift out from the Epistles what, by the exercise of his critical insight, he judged to be spurious, making the Epistles to the Corinthians (which he assumed to be beyond question genuine) the touchstone by which he tested the genuineness of everything else. He went further than F. C. Baur in ejecting suspicious portions from some of the Epistles, but acknowledged as genuine the greater part, not only of the

---

[1] *Kritik der paulinischen Briefe.* Berlin 1852.
[2] *Beiträge zur Kritik der paulinischen Briefe.* Leipzig 1867.

four first Epistles, but also of those to the Philippians and the Colossians. His criticism, however, seemed so arbitrary that he found no followers.

Dutch critics were the first, after Bruno Bauer, to question the genuineness of all of Paul's Epistles. Allard Pierson, in a discussion of the Sermon on the Mount (published in 1878) expressed incidentally serious doubt whether the common assumption of the Pauline authorship of the Epistle to the Galatians could be maintained. Later (1882 *sqq.*) another Dutchman, A. D. Loman, took up the subject of Paul's Epistles in a theological periodical, and combated the genuineness of the whole of them. Still more recently Pierson, this time in combination with a philologist, S. A. Naber [1], has discussed the subject at large, taking the ground that the Epistles were for substance Jewish productions, the authors, however, being regarded as Jews of a more spiritual sort than the most. These writings he assumes that a Christian redactor, whom he calls Paulus Episcopus, put together and supplemented, so that all that is distinctively and unmistakably Christian in them must be attributed to him. This result is, to be sure, widely different from that of Bruno Bauer. The latter regarded Judaism as having much less influence on primitive Christianity than the Tübingen school maintained, and considered the Epistles to have been of purely Christian origin. Moreover, he divided the Epistles differently. The Epistle to the Romans, for example, he deemed to have been made

---

[1] *Verisimilia*. Amsterdam 1886.

up of only four distinct parts, namely, chapters i.—viii., chapters ix.—xi., chapters xii.—xiv., and chapters xv., xvi. Pierson, on the contrary, holds the Epistle to have been mostly of Jewish origin, and to consist of a large number of Jewish fragments pieced together and supplemented by Paulus Episcopus.

A German scholar (though living in Switzerland) has at length been found to take up the long neglected work of Bruno Bauer. Professor Rudolf Steck of Berne, in a work[1] primarily devoted to the Epistle to the Galatians, discusses the whole question of the Pauline Epistles, and comes to the conclusion that they are all spurious. He agrees with Bruno Bauer on the main point. As to the Epistle to the Romans, he also agrees with him in the division of it into four parts, but disagrees with him in some matters of detail. He argues that there are insoluble difficulties besetting the assumption of the Pauline authorship of the Epistles; that they show manifest acquaintance with the Gospels; that they exhibit evidences of the influence of apocryphal and heathen writers whom Paul himself could not have been acquainted with; and that they betray a knowledge of customs which must have been unknown to Paul (e. g. 1 Cor. xv. 29)[2].

---

[1] *Der Galaterbrief nach seiner Echtheit untersucht, nebst kritischen Bemerkungen zu den paulinischen Hauptbriefen.* Berlin 1888.

[2] Still later has appeared a new discussion of the question by Prof. Daniel Völter of Amsterdam, *Die Komposition der paulinischen Hauptbriefe,* Tübingen 1890. Some comments on this will be made at a later point.

It is not to be expected that this radical rejection of views heretofore held by the conservative and by the liberal alike will at once carry conviction to all. But nothing can be clearer than that Steck's position is the logical outcome of the movement initiated by the Tübingen school. As we have remarked above, Baur's position was essentially untenable; and, as over against his orthodox opponents, the victory certainly cannot be accorded to him. The correct and consistent course would have been to assume the unhistorical character of the whole New Testament, to throw the *onus probandi* upon the opposing party, and then to strengthen and (so far as necessary) to defend this position in detail. For the fundamental principle of this criticism (though not always distinctly stated) is really such that the credibility of the Biblical books in general must be denied. When, therefore, any of these books is not anonymous, its genuineness must be contested, unless the author is regarded as a gross deceiver.

There are three assumptions, which we may regard as incontrovertible, lying at the foundation of all scientific criticism of the Bible. They are (1) that all important institutions are the result of a gradual growth; (2) that no miracle has ever taken place, and that supernaturalism is a superstition; (3) that all traditional opinions of a religious nature are to be assumed to be doubtful or false, except as they are confirmed by the general approval of critics. It is only when we make these assumptions that we can be genuinely critical and free from prepossessions. Now it follows at once and necessarily from these principles, that Christianity was of gradual growth, and owed nothing to startling or miraculous events or personages. And therefore it follows further that all the so-called Pauline Epistles are unauthentic, since they represent Jesus as an altogether unique and superhuman being, and Christianity as of supernatural origin. But if unauthentic, then the Epistles must be spurious, unless (what hardly any one would pretend) Paul was a shameless liar and impostor. This is the short method which a clear-headed and consistent criticism must adopt. And strictly speaking, the main question is thus settled at once. The course which the critical process takes depends on this fundamental assumption. It is, therefore, in reality hardly necessary to undertake to prove, by a minute examination of details the spuriousness of the Pauline Epistles. Still, as the astronomer finds a new satisfaction in seeing how each of the celestial phenomena harmonises with the fundamental principles of the Copernican and Newtonian system, so the critical student may rejoice when he sees that a close study of the doctrinal and linguistic characteristics of the New Testament books confirms the general conclusion already reached respecting the origin of Christianity. Besides, some minds are so peculiarly constituted that they require an accumulation of proofs, even when proof enough has already been furnished. Therefore it is well to show not only that the so-called Pauline Epistles *cannot be* genuine, but that they *are not* genuine. But for the present we take up only one of them — the most important one — the Epistle to the Romans. If an impartial and critical examination of this work shows that it is not what it has commonly been reputed to be, then assurance will have been made doubly sure, and one of the last strongholds of supernaturalism will have been captured.

The method to be pursued will be that of a critical analysis which, by showing that the Epistle is a composite work, written by at least four authors, each (or at least three) of them professing to be Paul, destroys the traditional conception root and branch. It has been a fault of critics hitherto that they have too largely assumed the *unity* of the several Epistles of the New Testament. And even as to the other books of the New Testament the critical partition which is accomplishing such noteworthy results in the Old Testament has not been undertaken to any great extent. The Gospels, it is true, are regarded as a compilation; but no thoroughly scientific analysis of their contents has yet been made which presents us with a history of their growth at all comparable with the marvellous analysis and history of the Pentateuch which modern criticism has produced. A beginning has been made, as we have seen, with the Epistles; but it can hardly be called more than tentative. A more vigorous effort has recently been made to dissolve the Apocalypse into its original elements, though the two principal workers in this field do not agree in their result — the one[1] maintaining that the book

---

[1] Eberhard Vischer, *Die Offenbarung Johannis eine jüdische Apokalypse in christlicher Bearbeitung*. 1886.

in its main stock was of Jewish origin, and was afterwards worked over by Christian hands; the other[1] contending that the several parts, though the product of different periods, are all of Christian origin. But disagreements and unsuccessful experiments should not be permitted to retard the onward march of criticism. Sooner or later the right man with the sure insight will be found, who will discern the true make-up of each Biblical book so perfectly, and set it forth so clearly, that thenceforth his analysis will be accepted as the ultimate solution. It is with no small degree of confidence that the following analysis of the Epistle to the Romans is presented to the world as one which will at once commend itself to all candid minds as unmistakably correct. Even though future critics should need to modify our results in some unessential particulars, the analysis in its main features must be regarded as final. Let us then proceed to our work.

---

[1] Daniel Völter, *Die Entstehung der Apokalypse.* 1882. *Die Offenbarung Johannis keine ursprünglich jüdische Apokalypse* (a reply to Vischer). 1886.

CHAPTER II.

THE DOCTRINAL ARGUMENT.

The principal proof of diversity of authorship in any work must come from the detection of different types of thought in it. The more external features are of themselves insufficient to guide us. In our Epistle, for example, the singular fact that it has several apparent endings has long been remarked upon, and received all sorts of explanations. That a single writer should have left his letter with such a jumble of doxologies, benedictions, and salutations at the close seems very improbable. Yet such a thing is not absolutely impossible, though one's mind is relieved, when other and more decisive reasons are found for regarding the Epistle as made up of four distinct ones, so that the several endings belong to different authors, the compiler simply leaving them as he found them.

These four authors being themselves all unknown, we designate them for convenience' sake as G^1, G^2, JC, and CJ. We use the signs G^1 and G^2 for the reason that in the sections belonging to the first two there is almost no mention of Jesus Christ, but only of God, as the supreme authority and the author of salvation. They differ, however, decidedly in their theological drift. The terms JC and CJ are derived from the circumstance that in the sections belonging to the former the Redeemer is called Jesus Christ, but in those belonging to the latter, Christ Jesus. This distinction between the two is largely obliterated in the Textus Receptus, but comes out strikingly in the corrected text and in the Revised Version.

Let us now notice more in detail the characteristics of the four different writers. They are all Christians, but present different phases of Christian thought and doctrine. G[1] portrays Christianity as an ethical institution, a spiritualised Judaism. Salvation, according to him, is gained by *obedience to the law*. We find here nothing about *faith* of any sort as a condition of salvation. In G[2], on the contrary, though nothing is said about *faith in Jesus*, salvation is emphatically represented as a divine gift, and the appropriation of it comes through *faith in God* on the part of man. In JC the prominent thought is that of justification through *faith in Christ*, and particularly in Christ as a *vicarious sacrifice*. In CJ the chief stress is laid on the necessity of spiritual *union between the Christian and Christ*, through which the life of the flesh is replaced by that of the Spirit.

It will be most convenient for the reader to be able to see at once a statement of the conclusion to which our critical analysis has brought us. We divide the Epistle as follows:

G¹.	G².	JC.	CJ.
i. 18—ii. 15.	iii. 1—20.	i, 1—17.	vi. 2—vii. 6.
ii. 17—29.	iii. 27—iv. 24.	ii. 16.	viii. 1—39.
xii. 9-xiii. 13.	vii. 7—24.	iii. 21—26.	xii. 1—8.
xvi. 17—20.	ix. 6—33.	iv. 25—v. 21.	xiii. 14-xv. 7.
	xi. 1—36.	ix. 1—5.	xv. 14—33.
		x. 1—21.	xvi. 1—16.
		xv. 8—13.	
		xvi. 21—27.	

1. Let us begin with G¹. Of course the original production could not have begun so abruptly as this. The Redactor (whom we designate by R), having thought best to make an extract from JC the introduction, naturally omitted what originally served as the opening of G¹'s treatise. Of course the γάρ in i. 18 was inserted by R in order to effect an apparent connection between this and the preceding. "Apparent", we may well say; for, narrowly considered, the "for" is anything but appropriate. In verses 15—17 the writer (giving himself out as Paul) proclaims himself as the preacher of the gospel in which is revealed a righteousness of God by faith — a faith by which we are to live. How incongruous, now, the following is with this: The saving righteousness of God is revealed, *for* the wrath of God is revealed! And in all that follows in i. 18—ii. 29 we find not one word more about the justifying faith which has been announced as the burden of the writer's message, but only the divine vengeance on sinners, the deep depravity of

the heathen world, and the assurance that God will deal with men according to their works (ii. 6), both Jew and Gentile alike receiving even-handed justice (ii. 9—12). Manifestly this section is no continuation of what is introduced in i. 8—17. Here, on the contrary, the doctrine is laid down that *justification comes from works:* "the doers of a law shall be justified" (ii. 13). The whole burden of the section is that the world in general is corrupt and exposed to divine judgment, that men shall be judged by law (ii. 12), whether the law of their hearts (ii. 15) or the law of Moses. Circumcision is of no avail unless one keeps the law (ii. 25). If the uncircumcised keep the ordinances of the law, their uncircumcision is reckoned for circumcision (ii. 26). Throughout i. 18—32 the leading thought is that the nations by their corruption have exposed themselves to the divine wrath; in ch. ii. the thought is emphasized, that one should not judge another, that Jews should not blame Gentiles, since all are under one condemnation in so far as they are sinful. — This writer, however, though he lays stress on the law and the necessity of obeying it, is no Pharisee, insisting on outward forms and petty rules. Circumcision is declared to be unable to secure salvation; a right inward spirit is pronounced to be the essential thing. The law which he enjoins is the law of purity, of godliness, of love. But he has nothing whatever to say of Jesus Christ as an agent in the work of securing justification.

Having laid down his general doctrine and enforced it, G[1] concludes with some practical injunctions. According to our analysis these admonitions begin at xii. 9. This may seem arbitrary, as ch. xii. appears to be a connected series of exhortations. And the connection between ii. 29 and xii. 9 may seem very abrupt. This latter objection is well taken. But in reply it is only necessary to observe that R may have omitted what originally served as a transition, since he had decided to begin the hortatory part with a selection from CJ. Of course, therefore, G"'s introduction to the exhortations would necessarily drop out. But this being conceded, it may still be asked why just this section (xii. 9—xiii. 13) is assigned to G^1. Our reason is twofold: (1) the total absence of the name of Christ, and (2) the contents of the section. There runs through the whole of it the spirit of i. 18—ii. 29. The exhortations have reference to the moral law — the duty of love, of generosity, of forgiveness, of obedience to magistrates, of general compliance with the law of the two tables. God is still held up as the avenger (xii. 19, xiii. 2). But in all this Jesus is nowhere mentioned as the goal of effort or as the source of inspiration. More particularly, observe that xii. 1—8 is permeated by a different cast of thought. The prominent thing there is the union between Christ and his followers, and the union of believers with one another. The union with Christ involves the possession of gifts — *charismata* (xii. 6—8). What follows is indeed not inappropriate here; and R was skilful in inserting this section in this place. Yet a close scrutiny detects here a different atmosphere. Whereas in xii. 1—8 the underlying thought is that of the transformation of spirit which characterises the Christian (xii. 2) and the divine gifts which are bestowed in Christ (xii. 5, 6), in xii. 9—xiii. 13 the prevailing thought is that of the duties which men owe not only to fellow-Christians, but to all men. At xiii. 10 the thought culminates in the exalted statement, "Love is the fulfilment of the law". The author, however, goes on to make a more specific application of his admonitions by warning against sensuality and schism (xiii. 11—13). At ver. 14 we meet again with a sentiment characteristic of the mystical CJ, to whom belongs also ch. xiv. and the greater part of ch. xv. It is true that ver. 14 seems to follow the foregoing pertinently; and the exhortation to "put on" the Lord Jesus Christ might seem to betoken the same author who has just exhorted his readers to "put on" the armor of light (ver. 12). But, over against the manifest difference, all this only shows the skill of the redactor in weaving the documents together.

It may not be possible to prove with rigid conclusiveness whether any more of the Epistle was written by G[1]. As already observed, chh. xiv. and xv. are to be ascribed to others. Ch. xvi. is not of such a sort that the internal evidence is everywhere altogether decisive. It is, however, manifestly composite; ver. 16 constitutes an ending, and the next four verses (17—20) follow the salutations of verses 1—16 so inappropriately that they must have originated with a different author. And the burden of these verses (dissuasion from contention) is so appropriate as a continuation of xiii. 12, 13 that we can hardly be mistaken in assuming that these also are to be ascribed to G^1, and that with ver. 20 his part of the Epistle closes. It might be thought that the expression in ver. 18, "they that are such serve not the Lord Christ", is not characteristic of G^1, he having nowhere previously so much as even mentioned the name of Jesus. If one choose, he can of course eliminate this clause as being an interpolation, especially as the phrase "Lord Christ" nowhere else occurs in the Epistle, and seldom elsewhere. This latter consideration, however, might be urged on the other side, and the phrase regarded as distinguishing G^1 from the other authors. And after all there is no decisive reason for thinking that G^1 could not have so spoken of Jesus Christ. He probably wrote at a time when Jesus' authority had acquired a great prominence, though he had not come to be regarded as superhuman. But it is not at all inconceivable that, as being the founder of the Christian Church, the promulgator of a purified conception of the Mosaic law, Jesus may by this time have been spoken of as one who was to be *served*, just as Moses was often represented as one who had given commands (Mark x. 5) and was to be obeyed. — It is more doubtful whether the benediction in xvi. 20 is an original part of G^1. This form of benediction hardly accords with the general absence in G^1 of reference to Christ. If that view of Jesus' theanthropic nature which ultimately prevailed in Christendom had been shared by G^1, he would have made frequent reference to him. From internal evidence we infer that G^1 wrote not far from 80—90 A. D), when we may suppose that legendary influences had magnified the reputation of Jesus so that he was idealised and held to be a great authority, though doubtless not yet regarded as superhuman. Probably, therefore, such benedictions as that of xvi. 20 could hardly yet have been used; yet since R could have had no sufficient reason for interpolating it here, the most probable supposition is that this benediction had been added by some transcriber previous to R, in order to give the letter a proper termination, and that R simply left it as he found it. It may seem strange that R should not have omitted the benediction, however, so as to prevent the appearance of so many different endings to one letter. So we might ask, why did he leave xv. 33? Why did he allow the salutations to follow that benediction? However inexplicable all this may seem, it is certainly no more inexplicable than that Paul, or any other single author, should originally have put his letter into the form which it now has. It is easier certainly to suppose that R simply left the benedictions as he found them, and so, when he wove the different letters together, left an appearance of terminations followed by an addition to the Epistle, than that a single author should without any reason have introduced such a puzzling feature into his Epistle. It may be added, as another reason for doubting whether G^1 wrote this benediction, that the word χάρις, though frequently used by each of the other three writers, nowhere else occurs in G^1.

Whatever may be the fact concerning such incidental points, the main division we have made must be accepted as incontrovertible. G¹, as any one can see who reads consecutively the sections attributed to him, has a character quite distinct from either of the other three. In his general drift he closely resembles the author of the so-called Epistle of James. In both of them practical morality of an elevated kind is the aim of the writing. In both of them Jesus is mentioned with reverence, but very seldom, and rather as the propounder of a spiritual code of morals than as an object of personal faith and as the giver of spiritual life. In both of them faith denotes merely the acceptance of the Christian ethics as the rule of life. Cf. James ii. 1 with Rom. xiii. 11. James combats the notion that faith can have any other meaning and use. He must have written after this theological sense of the word had come into vogue, and therefore may have flourished somewhat later than G¹. But the two strikingly agree in their spirit. According to both justification comes from works, not from faith (Rom. ii. 13, James ii. 24). Both warn against a hearing of the word which is not accompanied by a doing of it (Rom. ii. 13, James i. 22). But James dwells more on certain special moral duties, whereas G¹ is more general and summary in his ethical injunctions.

It will have been noticed that in ch. ii. one verse has been dropped out as not belonging to G¹, viz., ver. 16. Our reason for this is not merely the fact that the name of Jesus Christ here occurs. The verse has always been a puzzle to commentators because it has no natural or easy connection with the context. It is, rhetorically considered, out of place, and numerous unsuccessful efforts have been made to explain it. But we shall notice this further at a later point.

2. We turn now to G^2. Here, too, the introduction, whatever it may have been, has been necessarily omitted, in order to connect the writing with that of G^1. The latter having spoken (ii. 28, 29) of the character of the true Jew, R skilfully inserts here a discussion from another source concerning the privileges and distinction of the Jews. But here we meet at the very outset with what is wholly wanting in G^1, namely, a reference to *faith* (iii. 3); and throughout ch. iv. G^2 is occupied with the proof and illustration of Abraham's faith. Quite in contrast with G^1, who not only nowhere speaks of faith, but expressly declares that justification comes from works, G^2 insists that faith is the subjective condition of salvation, God, however, not Christ, being the object of the faith and the sovereign dispenser of salvation. Whereas G^1 had argued that the heathen should be judged according to their works, G^2 argues that, just because the heathen are hopelessly corrupt, they can be saved only by divine grace, and not by the works of the law (iii. 20, 28, iv. 5). Nothing but the habit of indolent acquiescence in traditional notions can account for the fact that writings so opposite in their tenor can so long have been assumed to be the production of the same mind. A critical glance discerns the distinction, and every unbiased mind must

accept the verdict that two distinct authors are to be here detected.

The section iii. 21—26 is manifestly from a still different source. Faith is here portrayed quite otherwise than in the context. It is here faith in Christ and in his atoning blood. If it should be said that the *general* description of faith might be specialised as faith in Jesus Christ, we must reply that in the following section (iii. 27—iv. 24) there is a return to the general faith in God and an utter absence of reference to the special relation of it to Jesus. Moreover, as soon as the parts are once detached from one another by the critical analysis, every one sees at once the real relation of the passages. Throw out the verses (21—26) in which the name of Jesus abounds, whereas before and after it is wanting, and we not only eliminate the name, but we find that the connection of thought is made decidedly more clear and consistent. At iii. 19, 20 the author had concluded that every mouth is to be stopped, and that all the world is to be brought under the judgment of God. How naturally now does he add (iii. 27), "Where then is the glorying?" It is plain that R aimed to weave together the discourses of G^2 and JC. And there are indeed similarities which make the combination easy. Both lay stress on faith; both insist that justification is conferred apart from works of the law. But with G^2 the representation is that man becomes a child of God by virtue of faith that God will do what he has promised (iv. 13, 18, 20), whereas JC makes faith to be an acceptance of a redemption wrought out by Jesus through his sacrificial death.

G^2 furthermore is distinguished by the stress he lays on the divine sovereignty. He everywhere insists that God must have his way, whatever men may do. At the very outset (iii. 3) we find him saying, "What if some were without faith? Shall their want of faith make of none effect the faithfulness of God?" Every mouth must be stopped, and all the world must be brought under the judgment of God (iii. 19), who "calleth the things that are not as though they were" (iv. 17). This doctrine of the divine sovereignty is made still more prominent in ix. 6—33, where it is carried to the extreme of making God purely arbitrary in the bestowment of his favors (*vid.* verses 16, 20, 23). In ch. xi. also the same doctrine is emphasized. Divine grace and election are made the determining element in salvation and condemnation (cf. verses 5—8, 28, 29, 35, 36). Nowhere else in all the Epistle do we find this doctrine brought out. In chh. ix. and xi. we trace the same mind that produced chh. iii. and iv. with a certainty that can hardly be gainsaid. It is a question for exegetes, just how G^2 conceived the relation of divine sovereignty to human faith. For he everywhere lays stress also on this faith (iii. 28—31, iv. 5, 11—16, 20, ix. 30—32, xi. 20, 23). It is clear, however, that as compared with either of the three other authors he magnifies the absoluteness of the divine will.

But we must return a little. We have made the second section of G^2 end with iv. 24. That ver. 25 does not belong in it is clear from its character. It breathes the spirit of JC, and is wholly different from the preceding. But it may be questioned whether the last part of ver. 24 belongs to G^2. For here we find mention of Jesus and his resurrection. This, however, might conceivably be made by G^2. We cannot affirm that he did not believe in the resurrection of Christ. He certainly nowhere else speaks of it and must have attached little importance to it. It may be remarked, however, that in any case Jesus is not here represented as the object of faith, as is done by JC. It is still God in whom Christians are said to believe; only it is God "who raised Jesus from the dead". But on the whole it is by far most probable that this clause is an interpolation introduced by R to effect a transition to the JC section which he here inserts (v. 1—21). For even if we assume (what is indeed possible) that G^2 shared the legendary notion of the resurrection of Jesus, the introduction of this reference to it is, when narrowly considered, very awkward and pointless. He has been arguing from Abraham's case to that of his readers. Because Abraham's faith was reckoned to him for righteousness, therefore ours will be. There being this parallel, we should expect that, as Abraham's faith was simply a faith in God and his promises, so ours must be also. How inconsequent, therefore, it is to say that, as Abraham was justified because he believed in God, so we shall be justified if we believe in *the* God who raised Jesus from the dead! It can hardly be doubted that G^2 himself ended the sentence with πιστεύουσιν — "for the sake of us also, unto whom it shall be reckoned, who believe".

We come now to vii. 7—24. which we have designated as the next section belonging to G². It needs but little perspicacity to discern that this section interrupts the course of thought found in vi. 1—vii. 6, and resumed in ch. viii. But R could probably find no better place for it. It may be doubted whether originally it followed immediately after iv. 24. Possibly something was omitted here as not fitting easily into the connection. Yet there is no reason to assume the omission of any considerable portion. The connection between iv. 9—24 and vii. 7 *sqq.* is not obscure at all. G² has maintained that no one is justified by the works of the law. He has affirmed (iv. 15) that the law works wrath, and that salvation cannot be obtained by the works of the law (iii. 20, 28, iv. 16). It is, therefore, quite natural that the objection should occur to one: If this is so, then the law seems to be worse than useless; it serves to promote sin, and not to prevent it. And so the author must heed the objection. Accordingly he says (vii. 7): "What shall we say then? Is the law sin?" And then follows a discussion of the working of the law, in which the emphasis lies on the point that the law sharpens the conscience and develops a consciousness of moral evil, but does not deliver from the bondage of sin. All this connects admirably with chh. iii. and iv., but very poorly with ch. v., where the prominent thought is that of salvation through faith in Christ, or with ch. vi., where the author (CJ) dwells on the personal union between Christ and Christians — in neither of which chapters is any stress laid on the law, but faith is contrasted with sin, and salvation is represented as the gift of divine grace. G^2, however, magnifies the divine sovereignty; and now that he has directed attention to this apparently insuperable objection (that the law is a means of evil), he meets it, not by saying that repentance and faith in an atonement on man's part can secure salvation, but by the bold assertion that salvation is a divine gift conferred purely on the ground of sovereign election, not through Christ's death. After the impassioned exposition of the struggle between conscience and impulse, he ends by exclaiming, "Oh, wretched man that I am! Who shall deliver me from the body of this death?" The answer which immediately follows in ver. 25 is manifestly not from G^2. This whole verse is an interpolation, and serves only to connect vii. 7—24 with ch. viii. Strictly speaking, R interpolated only the first part of the verse. The last clause, instead of leading forward to the main thought of ch. viii., recurs to the general burden of vii. 7—24. R could hardly have done his work so awkwardly, if he had found nothing of this sort before him. Now, as we read the concluding words of ver. 25 attentively, we cannot but be struck with the fact that they are not at all in keeping with the passionate tone of the preceding. They sound rather like a cold summarizing of the general burden of the foregoing description. It is therefore most likely that some transcriber wrote this sentence on the margin, that a later one inserted it into the text, and that R finding it there did not eject it. This relation of things becomes obvious as soon as we clearly discern that vii. 7—24 is an interruption of the train of thought found in vi. 2—23 and viii. 1—39 and comes from a different source.

Having discovered this disturbing section to be from G^2, and the continuation of ch. iv., when we cast about for G^2's own answer to the despairing question of vii. 24, we find, as might have been expected, that it is not answered by G^2 as R and CJ answer it. He makes God, not Christ, the deliverer. And the bondage complained of in vii. 7—24 is removed, according to him, by divine power acting sovereignly. This is set forth in the next section belonging to G^2, namely ix. 6—33. Having pictured the desperate condition of the sinful man, whom the law seems to hurt more than help, he now gives the solution. Although the law of God, seems to do no good, yet, he says (ix. 6), "it is not as though the word of God hath come to nought". This is just the turn which the doleful conclusion of vii. 24 requires, and exactly harmonises with G^2's whole course of thought. And now follows this remarkable section, in which human agency is reduced, as it were, to the minimum, and the divine election is exalted as the ultimate arbiter of human destiny. That it is G^2, and not G^1, who is writing appears clearly when we find at the close that faith on man's part is still held up as necessary to the obtaining of the blessing (ix. 30—33). In the distinction between Abraham's seed and Abraham's children (ix. 6, 7) we recognise the same mind which uttered itself at iv. 11—17. Throughout chh. ix. and xi. the doctrine is drawn out, that salvation is for Jews and Gentiles alike, and that it is a gift of God appropriated by faith. But in all this not one word is said about Christ's death, or faith in his blood, or union with him — in fact not one word about Christ at all. No doubt G² recognised Jesus as an eminent teacher; but what Jesus taught was, according to him, that God himself is the Saviour and executes all his designs with sovereign power. In ch. xi. the author takes up more particularly the question about the Jews, and expresses the confident hope that Israel will finally obtain salvation, and in view of the prospect breaks out into the passionate exclamation, "Oh the depth of the riches both of the wisdom and the knowledge of God!" and ends with the doxology, "To him be glory for ever. Amen." This is manifestly *one* of the terminations of the Epistle. What follows has obviously no immediate connection with the foregoing. The "therefore" is inserted by R to give the appearance of sequence; but the exhortations of ch. xii. have evidently nothing in particular to do with the preceding discussion, and come from a different source.

3. We come now to JC. This author represents a decidedly different type of thought from G² or G¹. He must have lived at a time when Jesus had gained a unique authority, and was regarded as in a peculiar sense the mediator between God

and man. The influence of the Old Testament is still strong, however, but discloses itself in the representation of Jesus' death as the fulfilment of the Mosaic sacrifices. We may not improbably conjecture that he wrote about 120—130 A. D. Like G^2 JC emphasizes faith; but it is faith in Christ and his gospel. Jesus is at the outset glorified as the Son of God (i. 4). The chief emphasis is put on Christ's death and resurrection as the ground of the salvation which man receives through faith. Such a notion of Christ and his work can of course not have existed in the time of Paul. The use of the name of Paul in the opening verse is therefore an instance of pseudonymy the object of which was to secure a readier acceptance for the teachings of the writer. To make this still more plausible, he gives the letter the appearance of having been addressed to the Roman church by dwelling fictitiously on the personal relations between him and the Roman Christians. In i. 16, 17 he gives utterance to his central thought, and grounds his doctrine of faith on an Old Testament passage, "The just shall live by faith". Now, as we have already seen, he cannot have proceeded as he is made to do by R. Instead of the gospel just announced as the central theme, we find nothing but law and wrath throughout the rest of this, and all the following, chapter. But in the midst of this long section there occurs one verse (ii. 16) which bears all the appearance of belonging to JC. It is every way a striking phenomenon; and though we may not be able to explain fully why R inserted it just here, in the midst of G^1's discourse, we can at any rate insist that on the theory of the Pauline authorship of the whole Epistle the phenomenon is no more easily explained. The verse has always puzzled the commentators. It has no apparent connection with the context. It is even inconsistent with it; for the accusing and excusing activity of conscience spoken of in ii. 15 is obviously something taking place *now*, not in the future day of judgment. The discovery that ii. 16 is by a different author from him who penned the context is the simple solution of the problem. The use of the name Jesus Christ just here, whereas it occurs nowhere in the context, and the fact that only here is any mention made of the gospel, make it practically certain that this is a sentence belonging to JC, but detached from its context. Whether deliberately by R, or accidentally in some other way, may be questioned. It may be that R had the feeling that in all this discussion G^1 betrays too little recognition of Christianity, that he therefore wished somewhere to insert a clause which would bring G^1 more obviously into the Christian line of thought, and that he found no better place than this[1]. It may not be possible to show where the verse originally belonged. In patching together

---

[1] This, whether or not the true reason, is at all events a better one than can always be given for the numerous similar dislocations in the Pentateuch. E. g. Gen. ii. 4 ᵃ, as the critics have pointed out, originally belonged before i. 1, but was transferred by R to this place. The fact of course no one can doubt; but can any one give a sufficient reason for the transference?

several treatises R must have omitted some passages altogether; and the immediate context of this verse may now be lost. Yet it is not difficult to suppose that the verse originally followed immediately after i. 17; only, in order to avoid the appearance of making the utterance in ii. 16 a part of the quotation from the Old Testament, we must assume that JC expressed himself somewhat like this: "As it is written, The just shall live by faith; that is to say, they shall live in the day when God shall judge", etc. Inasmuch as "live" in the New Testament is very often used tropically of the future life of blessedness (cf. John vi. 57, xiv. 19), this is a very appropriate combination.

The doctrine propounded at i. 16, 17 is not found again till we reach iii. 21—26. This section follows i. 1—17 naturally and admirably. Here again comes the doctrine of righteousness through faith; but it is more fully drawn out, and defined as faith in the atoning blood of Christ. Then follows the section iii. 27—iv. 24, already considered, which interrupts the discussion of the specific doctrine of JC, though it agrees with it in so far as faith is set over against salvation through works. But the next sentence from JC is found at iv. 25, which, without any change or addition perfectly connects with iii. 26, so that we read: "the justifier of him that hath faith in Jesus, who was delivered up for our trespasses, and was raised for our justification". Then follows ch. v., which unfolds the doctrine of free grace still further, and brings the discussion to an end. Chh. vi—viii., as already observed, belong to other writers.

We next come upon JC at ix. 1—5, where (still giving himself out as Paul) he gives utterance to the fervent wish that the Jews may become partakers of the great salvation. At ver. 5 occurs a doxology and an apparent conclusion. But this is, as has always been understood, only an exclamation bursting out of the deep emotion of the writer. Still it does mark a break. What follows, though on the same general topic, and not incongruous with the foregoing, is from another author, G^2, as already shown. From here to the end of the chapter there is no further use of the name of Jesus (an omission which in JC would have been impossible), and there is the same dwelling on Jewish history in which G^2 indulges in ch. iv. It is at x. 1 that we find the continuation of ix. 5. Let any one see for himself how much more appropriate and logical the connection is than between ix. 1—5 and the following. After expressing his grief on account of the Jews, "whose is the adoption and the glory", etc., JC goes on to say, "Brethren, my heart's desire and my supplication to God is for them, that they may be saved". Here is the obvious continuation of ix. 1—5. In ch. x. JC dwells on the mistake made by the Israelites in trying to establish a righteousness of their own and on the refusal of the larger part of them to listen to the glad tidings. He differs from G^2 as regards his anticipations respecting the future of the Jews. G^2 (in ch. xi.) expresses an assurance that eventually the covenant people will become partakers of the great salvation. JC, however, though fervently desirous of such a result, can only lament the obstinacy of the greater part of the Jews, quoting at the end (x. 21) the passage, "All the day long did I spread out my hands unto a disobedient and gainsaying people". Moreover, the dogmatic point of view is noticeably different in ch. x. from what it is in chh. ix. and xi. In the former stress is laid on man's faith. God saves those who call upon him (x. 9, 12, 13), and the salvation depends on faith in Christ (x. 4, 9). In the latter, though faith in God is represented as the medium of receiving salvation, the salvation is described as the gift of sovereign grace (ix. 15, 13, 24; xi. 2, 29, 32).

The next and final section of JC's part of the Epistle is xv. 8—13. Even a superficial glance at this chapter shows that this passage is out of place. The preceding exhortation to the strong to bear the burdens of the weak, and to be patient and harmonious in their Christian life, receives no illustration or support from the statement that Christ has been made a minister of the circumcision that he might confirm the promise given to the fathers. This has nothing to do with the foregoing, and quite as little to do with the following (xv. 14 *sqq.*). But it comes in admirably as a continuation and completion of ch. x. There he sets forth that the gospel was designed for the Jews, but had been largely rejected by them. Here he says that Christ is a minister of the circumcision for the truth of God in order to confirm the promises made to the Jews, and also that the Gentiles might glorify God for his mercy. What follows, however, are quotations from the Old Testament foreshadowing the gathering in of the Gentiles. How clearly we discern here the same mind as in i. 8—17, where also the gospel is declared to be for both Jew and Gentile, but where also the stress lies on the conversion of the Gentiles (verses 13, 14). If xv. 8—13 had been written by the same man who wrote ch. xi., he could not have been content to leave, as the final impression, that the ministry of Christ to the circumcision was to have, as its main outcome, only the ingathering of the Gentiles, the Jews themselves being tacitly relegated to unbelief and condemnation.

Ver. 13 is a benediction, which seems to come in rather abruptly, but of course no more abruptly on our hypothesis than on any other. It terminates the doctrinal part of JC's discourse, and it might be conjectured that JC's letter ended here. But it seems on the whole probable that he added the salutations of xvi. 21—23 and the final benediction, vers. 25—27. in which the name "Jesus Christ" occurs, and which therefore was presumably written by JC.

4. Finally we turn to CJ. As in the case of G^1 and G^2, the original beginning of CJ's Epistle was dropped, as being unnecessary; and we cannot conjecturally supply the deficiency. R was here more skilful than usual in putting his patchwork together. The question with which ch. vi. opens is naturally suggested by the course of thought at the close of ch. v., and what follows is an answer to the question. It is of course conceivable that in

what was omitted of CJ's production something occurred which made this question appropriate. But it is far more likely that the question was inserted by R in order to effect a transition from ch. v. to the Epistle of CJ. He had only to insert this question, which for substance was really used by CJ in vi. 15, in this place; and so an excellent connection was effected between the following and the foregoing.

That ch. vi. was not written by JC, however, is evident not merely or chiefly from the fact that the name of Jesus is here uniformly found in the form "Christ Jesus", but from the type of religious thought found in it. In JC the emphasis lies on the vicarious death of Christ (*vid.* iii. 25, v. 6—11); here, on the contrary, it is laid on the doctrine that the Christian dies to sin, *i. e.*, puts it away from him and is freed from its power. There the death of Christ is represented as a sacrificial death; here, rather, as an example which we have to follow (*vid.* vi. 8—11). There Jesus appears as the reconciling Mediator *through* whom and *from* whom justification and salvation are imparted to men (v. 11, 15, 16, 18, 21); here, rather, as he *in* whom men are made partakers of a new life (vi. 3—6, 11, 23). This general cast of thought is maintained throughout chh. vi., vii. 1—6, and viii. 1—39. Union with Christ in his spiritual life is the cardinal feature of the whole section. In the JC sections, on the contrary, this thought is not found at all.

The difference between the two writers strikingly appears in their different conception of *righteousness* and *justification*. Both of them use the term δικαιοσύνη, but not in the same sense. In every instance in which JC uses it (i. 17, iii. 21, 22, 25, 26, v. 17, 21, x. 3—6, 10) with reference to the peculiar state or privilege of the Christian, it is used in a forensic sense; it is God's justifying righteousness, an imputed righteousness, not a moral state of uprightness. CJ, on the contrary, in every instance uses the word to denote the moral or religious state of the Christian. He uses it at vi. 13, 16, 18, 19, 20, viii. 10, xiv. 17. No one looking at these passages by themselves, and without reference to JC's use of δικαιοσύνη, would ever think of assigning to the word here any other than the simple ethical sense. And even those who regard the Epistle as a unit have for the most part recognised this difference of sense. In reference to only one of these passages (vi. 16), does Meyer, for example, undertake to interpret the word as denoting justification; and in this case he makes it refer not to the present state, but to the final judgment. Such phrases as "the righteousness of God", "gift of righteousness", "righteousness which is of faith", are entirely wanting in CJ.

The same difference appears in the use of the verb δικαιόω, and the nouns δικαίωμα and δικαίωσις. The verb is used twice by JC (v. 1, 9) and both times expressly with reference to justification through faith in Christ's atonement. It is used four times by CJ (vi. 7, viii. 30 *bis*, 33), but in none of these instances is there any such express connection indicated. No doubt the verb in all these cases may have a forensic sense; but in none of them is the notion connected with the atonement of Christ. Δικαίωσις occurs only in JC (iv. 25, v. 18), and in both cases is used with express reference to justification through Christ's redeeming work. Δικαίωμα is used by both, but in an entirely different sense. JC (v. 16, 18) means by it a judicial sentence, or justifying act: CJ means by it simply an ordinance (viii. 4).

In short, the general conception concerning the initiation of the Christian life is markedly different in the two writers. According to JC it is introduced by faith in Christ on man's part (i. 17, iii. 22, 25. 26, v. 1, 2) and by an act of gracious acquittal on God's part (iii. 21, 24, 26, v. 9, 16, 17, 18, 21). According to CJ, however, the Christian life is begun by dying to sin, by being identified with Christ in his death to sin (vi. 2—11, vii. 6, viii. 2), and entering upon a spiritual life in Christ (vi. 11, 16, viii. 9—11, 14—17). It is a striking fact that, while JC speaks of faith (πίστις) in this specific sense of justifying faith in Christ's atonement no less than ten times (i. 17 tris, iii. 22, 25, v. 1, 2, x. 6, 8, 17), and of believing (πιστεύω) no less than eight times (i. 16, iii. 22, x. 4, 9—11, 14 bis) in the same sense, CJ *nowhere* in the dogmatic part of his work uses πίστις, and when he does use it, in the hortatory part (xii, 3, 6, xiv. 1, 23 bis), in every case denotes by it merely the general religious attitude of the Christian. This is equally true of his use of πιστεύω (vi. 8, xiv. 2), which, as he employs it, has no reference whatever to faith in Christ's atonement.

3*

Now if anything is cardinal in the so-called Pauline doctrines, it is the conceptions of faith and justification. Yet with reference to these conceptions we discover a marked and unmistakable distinction between JC and CJ. Their phraseology is largely different; and where it is identical the meaning is different. But let us now pass on to consider the remainder of CJ's part of the Epistle.

At vii. 7—24 we stumble, as already observed, upon a train of thought entirely different from what precedes and what follows. In this section we find nothing about Christ, nothing about justification, nothing about sanctification; but on the contrary there is described a condition of bondage to sin. Why R inserted the passage from G^2 just here may seem mysterious. But whatever may be conjectured as the reason, one thing is certain: there is no greater difficulty on our theory than on the traditional one. Why should *Paul* have interrupted his train of thought by such an irrelevant passage? Still there is at least an apparent connection. In vii. 6 sin and law seem to be identified, and the Christian state is described as a deliverance from both. This suggests the objection which is presented in vii. 7, although, as we have seen, this same objection is suggested by what is said in ch. iv. But the certain thing is that in its general spirit and drift this section is quite different from its surroundings. Ch. vi. describes the state of being made free from sin (verses 18—23). The same description continues through vii. 1—6. From there, if we omit vii. 7—25, the transition is as easy as possible.

The whole of chapter viii. is nothing but a development of the same general idea — freedom from sin and condemnation (verses 1—9), union with Christ (verses 10, 17, 35), and walking after or in the Spirit (verses 4, 5, 9, 11, 23, 26). At the close of the chapter the author concludes his doctrinal discussion in an eloquent burst of confident assurance of the indissolubleness of the union between the Christian and Christ.

There remain the exhortations and salutations which we have assigned to CJ. These begin at xii. 1—8. What is here enjoined breathes a spirit and is expressed in language strikingly like that of vi. 11—13. Closely cognate with the doctrine of the union of Christians with Christ is that of Christians with one another; and this is here urgently enforced (xii. 4, 5). As already observed, it may seem to be somewhat arbitrary to assign xii. 9 *sqq.*, to another author. There seems to be no marked change of style or tone at this point. The exhortations of xii. 9 — xiii. 13 are in general harmony with those of xii. 1—8. The injunctions, to shew mercy with cheerfulness, and to let love be without hypocrisy, are certainly kindred; and R was unusually happy in his dovetailing here. But, as we remarked before, the general cast of thought is after all not the same in the two sections. It is scarcely conceivable that CJ could have written so much without once using the name of Christ. The central thought of xii. 9 — xiii. 13 is that of *obedience to law*, but to law in its spiritualised form — the law of love. The central thought of xii. 1—8 is that of the union of Christians with one another in Christ[1]. This thought re-appears in ch. xiv. This whole chapter, as also xv. 1—7, deals with the duty of Christians to one another as common members of the body of Christ, especially as related to the question of receiving new members and the proper mode of dealing with weak members. The last verse of ch. xiii. probably belongs to CJ, although it does not appear to be a specially happy transition from xiii. 11—13 to xiv. 1. But G^1 could not have written the verse. The notion of putting on the Lord Jesus and not making provision for the flesh is entirely in the spirit of CJ; and if the verse was not originally found at this point, we must suppose that its context was dropped, and this particular verse was retained by R as coming in appropriately after xiii. 13 and as furnishing a good conclusion to this class of admonitions.

The hortatory part of CJ closes at xv. 7. The section xv. 8—13, as already remarked, and as is obvious at a glance, has nothing to do with the preceding, and belongs to JC. In xv. 14—33, however, we detect again the hand of CJ. The name of Jesus, when joined with the epithet Christ is in the form "Christ Jesus". The author here speaks more of his personal relations to the readers and of his personal activity. Though the name of Paul is not used, it is clear enough that he means to give

---

[1] It was not till after our critical inspection of the Epistle had detected this distinction that we noticed that Tischendorf makes a new paragraph begin at xii. 9.

himself out as Paul. At ver. 33 we have a benediction which might seem to be the end of CJ's part of the Epistle; but the following salutations (xvi. 1—16) are almost certainly to be ascribed to CJ. The form "Christ Jesus" (ver. 3), and the frequent use of the phrase "fellow-worker *in* Christ" etc., are characteristic of CJ. so that this section is to be regarded as an appendix.

We have now gone through the whole Epistle, and unmistakably shown that, when its contents are examined, they disclose themselves as the product of at least four different minds. To the unprejudiced the arguments must be ample. But that the proof may be complete, we will consider the evidence to be derived from the language of the Epistle.

CHAPTER III.

THE LINGUISTIC ARGUMENT.

1. WE have had frequent occasion to call attention to the striking fact that certain parts of the Epistle are characterized by the use of the name Jesus Christ, others by the use of the form Christ Jesus, while in still others the name of Jesus scarcely occurs at all. In the sections which we have assigned to JC the form "Christ Jesus" occurs only once (iii. 24). When we consider how the Textus Receptus has almost obliterated the distinction between the two forms, the copyists in their carelessness having substituted one for the other, it is not strange that in a single case such a substitution should have found its way into the earlier MSS., and no trace be found of the original form. Of course we cannot affirm that JC himself could not once have used the form Christ Jesus. But when we consider how uniformly in certain long sections the one form, and in others the other, prevails, it seems most likely that this single exception is due

to transcribers rather than to the author. In the passages assigned to CJ we never find the simple form "Jesus Christ". Thrice, however, he uses the combination "Lord Jesus Christ" (xiii. 14, xv. 6, 30). But the form "Lord Christ Jesus" never occurs anywhere, so that this is scarcely to be regarded as an exception.

Now it may be objected that the difference between "Jesus Christ" and "Christ Jesus" is a purely rhetorical one, and cannot be regarded as betokening difference of authorship. Could not the same man use interchangeably both forms? This certainly is quite conceivable. But when we find the one form used exclusively in sections of considerable length, and then the other exclusively in other sections; moreover, when we find the distinction *coinciding with a clear distinction in doctrinal type*, then it is no longer reasonable to assume that the variation is a mere unmeaning accident. When we find that the mystic, CJ, uniformly uses the combination "Christ Jesus", while the theologian, JC, uniformly uses the other. the peculiarity in the use of the names confirms the conclusion already arrived at on the ground of the difference in doctrinal thought. But why should the one prefer the one name, and the other the other? Even if we could not tell, the argument from the distinction would be no less valid. But we can at least give a conjectural explanation. In the form "Christ Jesus" the emphasis lies on the last word; and this form suits especially the writer who emphasizes the intimate and tender relation subsisting between Christ and his followers.

It need hardly be mentioned that all this is not inconsistent with the fact that both JC and CJ frequently use the term Christ alone. The variation in the use of the names of the Redemeer, if it stood by itself, would, however striking, not be sufficient to establish the proof of diverse anthorship. But when we find it running parallel with deeper differences, it becomes a strong proof. It is a second witness confirming the word of another.

2. The next point to which we call attention might have been treated when we spoke of the contents of the Epistle. We refer to the ethical use of the word σάρξ, flesh. The word has frequently, in the so-called Pauline Epistles, this peculiar meaning. But so far as the Epistle to the Romans is concerned, it is a striking fact that this special use of the word is confined to *one* of the four authors, *viz.*, CJ. It is manifest that this terminology is quite in harmony with the general style of CJ. His fundamental principle is that the Christian life is a new life in the Spirit, and radically distinguished from the old life which, as contrasted with the new, he calls living in the flesh. The term "flesh" occurs, it is .true, in other parts of the Epistle, but only in its more literal sense, *e. g.*, i. 3, ii. 28, iii. 20, iv. 1 etc. The ethical sense, of sinful passions and impulses, occurs only in vi. 19, vii. 5, viii. 3, 4, 5, 8, 9, 12 *bis*, 13, xiii. 14 — in every case, therefore, in the writings of CJ, while in all the other writers this sense is entirely wanting. Can this be a pure accident? To be sure, at vii. 18, 25 (in G²) we seem to find instances of the same ethical

sense. But there are ample reasons for judging that in these two verses this use of the word is to be attributed to R, who thus sought to bring this section as much as possible into connection with the context. We have already for other reasons concluded vii. 25 to be an interpolation. As for vii. 18, the clause, "that is, in my flesh", is manifestly superfluous, and sounds decidedly like an epexegesis added by another hand than that of the writer[1].

---

[1] No one can object to this critical conjecture who has had occasion to see how often the same process has to be resorted to by Old Testament critics, in order to keep the several constituent parts distinct. If this liberty were not allowed, there would often be serious embarrassment in disentangling the parts. *E. g.*, the critics agree in assigning Ex. i. 1—5 to P (Q), and i. 6 to J. But in verse 7, which is assigned to P, occur words which are characteristic of J, especially וישרצו. This, therefore, must be ejected. To be sure, the critics are not agreed as to the rest of the verse. Wellhausen *(Composition des Hexateuchs,* p. 62) throws out וירבו also; while Nöldeke retains this, and ejects וישרצו. The last two verbs are found in both P and J, the latter most frequently in P, though Wellhausen himself (p. 63) admits it in Ex. vii. 28 [Engl. viii. 3], which he assigns to JE. A more important instance of a similar critical procedure is found in 1 Sam. ii. 22, where the last part of the verse, on account of the occurrence of the phrase אהל מועד, has to be thrown out by the critics, because it conflicts with their theory that the tabernacle never existed except in the fancy of postexilic writers. Wellhausen *(Prolegomena zur Geschichte Israels,* p. 43) gives two reasons for doing so: (1) that the passage is "poorly attested", and (2) that "its contents are suspicious". The first is founded on the fact that the LXX does not contain the passage, though the Alex. Codex of the LXX and all other ancient versions contain it. But even if all the codices of the LXX had it, the second reason would be sufficient, and would

The same is to be said of the adjective σάρκινος (σαρκικός) in vii. 14. Indeed this whole verse is most probably an interpolation by R. The thought is only a repetition of that of verses 12 and 23. If we leave the verse out, it is not missed at all.

Moreover, it is to be observed that the antithesis of this ethical σάρξ is πνεῦμα. In the ethico-spiritual sense *this word also is found only in CJ*: cf. viii 4, 5, 6, 13. This word is in fact not found in the other three authors, except in i. 4, 9. ii. 29, v. 5. ix. 1, xi. 8, xii. 11, xv. 13; and in none of these cases does it have the peculiar sense. Now it is self-evident that the adjectives "fleshly" and "spiritual" could not have been used in the ethical sense till after the substantives were so used: and it is therefore extremely unlikely that G² could have used these two adjectives in such a sense while he nowhere so used the substantives. We can therefore hardly have any doubt that vii. 14 is wholly an interpolation.

This second point only serves to argue a distinction between CJ and the rest of the Epistle. The point previously considered served to argue a distinction between CJ and JC, and between these two and the rest of the Epistle. Thus far the

---

no doubt have led to the expulsion of the clause, even if there had been no other reason. In view of the indisputable right of critics to reject, as interpolations, words and phrases which are specially characteristic of another writer, we hardly need to give any other reason for our rejection of the clause in question in Rom vii. 18 than the simple fact that σάρξ is here found used in a sense which is characteristic of CJ.

linguistic argument at the best points to no more than three authors. We pass now, however, to a more minute linguistic analysis.

3. We have made a complete collation of all the words of the Epistle, excepting only a few of the most common words, such as θεός, the more frequent conjunctions and prepositions, the article, the numerals, the pronouns, and most proper names. We have tabulated them and can at a glance see where in each of the four authors, and how many times, each word is used.

We have found, besides the words above mentioned as left out, 928 words in the Epistle. Of these there are 173 used only by G^1, 171 by G^2, 98 by JC, and 186 by CJ. The sum of these is 628, so that there remain only 300 that are used in common by two or more of the four. In particular the relation is best seen when put into a tabular form.

Used only by G^1	173
" " " G^2	171
" " " JC	98
" " " CJ	186
" " " G^1 and G^2	25
" " " G^1 and JC	13
" " " G^1 and CJ	30
" " " G^2 and JC	31
" " " G^2 and CJ	40
" " " JC and CJ	31
" " " G^1, G^2, and JC	17
" " " G^1, G^2, and CJ	28
" " " G^1, JC, and CJ	15

Used only by G^2, JC, and CJ . 30
" by all four 40
Total 928

From this table we gather that G^1 uses in all 341 words, G^2 382, JC 275, and CJ 400. Consequently it follows that more than a half of the words used by G^1 are used by him alone, viz., 50.73 per cent. The proportion in the case of G^2 is 44.76; of JC, 35.64; of CJ, 44.

We should naturally expect the number of different words used to correspond pretty nearly with the whole number of words used, including repetitions of the same word. But this is not the case. Thus, while there are only 73 verses in the sections assigned to G^1, he uses 341 different words[1]. JC, on the other hand, who writes 85 verses, uses only 275 different words. Stated proportionally, the relation is as follows: G^1 uses (words 341, verses 73) 4.67 times more words than verses; G^2 (382 : 131) 2.92 times more; JC (275 : 85) 3.24 times more; CJ (400 : 142) 2.82 times more. In every respect, therefore, G^1 is the most unique of the four. He uses decidedly more words in proportion to the extent of his writings; he has a decidedly larger proportion of words used only by himself. G^2 and CJ are in these respects nearly alike. JC exceeds these two in the proportion of words to verses, but is the least original of all in the relative proportion of words used by himself alone. Between G^1 and

---

[1] It would be more exact to count the words (including repetitions) rather than the verses. But the proportion would not be materially different.

G^2, who might have been expected to present a similarity in their vocabulary and style, there is a marked difference. Is it conceivable that one and the same writer in the first half of his work would use 4.67 times more words than verses, and in the second half only 2.92 times more? Let us compare G^1 and JC as respects the words peculiar to each. In his 73 verses G^1 uses 173 words which occur nowhere else in the Epistle, *i. e.*, on the average 2.73 in every verse. JC, on the other hand, in his 85 verses uses only 98 words not found in the other parts; that is, on the average in every verse only 1.15! G^2 and CJ on the contrary, although theologically very unlike, come much nearer together in their vocabulary and in the proportion of words to verses. But we leave it to the reader to carry out the comparisons for himself.

It is instructive to compare this result with a similar analysis of Gen. i — xii. 5 which has been made by Prof. W. R. Harper[1]. He finds the whole number of different words to be 485, of which P uses 239, and J 367. Those used exclusively by P number 118, by J 246. Therefore there are 121 common to the two. Turning now to our Epistle and comparing G^1 and G^2, we find that together they use 613 different words, but that only 110 are common to the two. That is, while $1/4$ of the whole vocabulary of P and J is common to the two, only $\frac{1}{5.57}$ of the whole vocabulary of G^1 and G^2 is common to the two. So far as this indication goes, there-

---

[1] In the *Hebraica*, October 1888.

fore, it speaks more decidedly for the non-identity of G^1 and G^2 than for that of P and J. If we compare the whole number of different words used by P and J with the number used by each exclusively, it appears that those which P alone uses are $\frac{1}{4.11}$ of the whole, while those used by J alone are $\frac{1}{1.97}$ of the whole. This is a striking disproportion, but it is almost equalled by that which is found between CJ and JC, who together use 559 words, of which $\frac{1}{3}$ are used by CJ alone, but only $\frac{1}{5.70}$ by JC alone.

Let us now take JC and CJ. Together they use 559 different words. Common to the two only 116, that is $\frac{1}{4.82}$, as against the $\frac{1}{4}$ in the case of P and J.

If we compare similarly G^2 and CJ, we find that together they use 644 different words. Of these 138 are common to the two, that is, $\frac{1}{4.66}$ of the whole.

Comparing G^1 and CJ, we find that together they use 628 words, of which 113 are common to the two, that is, only $\frac{1}{5.58}$ of the whole.

Comparing G^1 and JC, we find that together they use 531 words, of which 85 are common to the two, that is, $\frac{1}{6.25}$ of the whole.

Comparing G^2 and JC, we find them using 539 words in all, and of these 118 in common, that is, $\frac{1}{4.57}$ of the whole.

We have thus gone through the possible permutations, and find that in the comparison of any two of these parts of the Epistle to the Romans with one another, the number of words common to the two is never more than $\frac{1}{4.57}$ of the whole, and in one case is only $\frac{1}{6.25}$ of the whole. the average being $\frac{1}{5.23}$, as over against the $\frac{1}{4}$ in the corresponding comparison of P and J in Gen. i—xii. 5. Every one must see the significance of this result. If the linguistic phenomena brought out by Prof. Harper indicate difference of authorship in Gen. i—xii. 5, *a fortiori* does the result of our analysis indicate the fourfold authorship of the Epistle to the Romans[1].

This general conspectus of the vocabulary of the Epistle might seem to be sufficient, in connection with the presentation of the doctrinal differences, to establish our main proposition beyond the

---

[1] Our omission of the pronouns and the more common conjunctions and prepositions must be quite balanced by the prefixes, suffixes, and inseparable prepositions and conjunctions of the Hebrew, which of course cannot have been counted in Prof. Harper's enumeration. Should all these words be added to our list, it would be increased by about 64, of which 41 are used by all in common. But here, too, striking phenomena appear. E. g., πρός occurs nowhere in G^1, once in G^2, but 7 times in JC and 10 times in CJ. "Ὅς is used by CJ 17 times, by G^2 13 times, but by JC only 4 times, and by G^1 only once. Οὕτω occurs 17 times in G^1 and nowhere else. Ἀπό occurs in CJ 15, in G^1 and JC each 4, in G^2 only 2 times. Ἐγώ in G^2 10, in CJ 4, in JC 2 times, in G^1 not at all. Εἰ in G^2 22, CJ 20, in G^1 and J each 4 times. Ἵνα in CJ 14, G^2 12, JC 4 times, in G^1 not at all. Μετά in CJ 4 times, JC twice, G^1 once, G^2 not at all. Μή interrogative in G^2 6 times, JC once, in G^1 and CJ not at all. Σύν 4 times in CJ, nowhere else. Τίς in G^2 24, CJ 14, JC 4 times, in G^1 not at all. Ὑπέρ in JC 10, CJ 8 times, G^2 once, G^1 not at all.

possibility of doubt. Is it rational to suppose that, if all these parts of the Epistle were written by one man, there would be so large a proportion of words used exclusively in each of the four parts? But we need not rest our argument on this general aspect of the case. Let us go more into particulars.

We cannot of course derive a conclusive argument from words which occur only once in the Epistle. Yet these cannot be thrown aside as of no weight at all. If the number of them were small, we should say that such a phenomenon is just what might have been expected; but if the number is very large, the case is radically different. When we find that *more than one half* of G^1's words are used in none of the other three parts, and that (though in a less proportion) each of the other three parts presents likewise an immense proportion of words found in none of the others, every one must see that in this there is an indication of diversity of authorship.

But let us take up the words that are used more than once. Here we may distinguish several classes.

a. When a word occurs more than once, but only in one of the four parts, we find in this fact a strong confirmation of the hypothesis that the four parts originated with different authors. Thus, to take the parts up in order, we find that the following words are used more than once, but only in G^1: φῶς and σκότος, ii. 19, xiii. 12; ἔπαινος, ii. 29, xiii. 3; τελέω, ii. 27, xiii. 6; ἀποδίδωμι, ii. 6, xii. 17, xiii. 7; φανερός, i. 19, ii. 28 (*bis*); τοιοῦτος, i. 32, ii. 2, 3,

xvi. 18; προσκαρτερέω, xii. 12, xiii. 6; μοιχεύω, ii. 22 (bis), xiii. 9; κλέπτω, ii. 21 (bis), xiii. 9; ἔρις, i. 29; xiii. 13; ἀναπολόγητος, i. 20, ii. 1; ἀτιμάζω, i. 24, ii. 23. It is noticeable how many of these are found in two widely separated sections which had been assigned to G¹ on the ground of the contents, before the linguistic examination was made.

In G² alone are found the following: ἀπιστία, iii. 3, iv. 20, xi. 20, 23; ἀποκτείνω, vii. 11, xi. 3; ἐκκλάω, xi. 17, 19, 20; ἐκλογή, ix. 11, xi. 5, 7, 28; ἐπεί, iii. 6, xi. 6, 22; μισέω, vii. 15, ix. 13; ὁδός, iii. 16, 17, xi. 33; ὀφθαλμός, iii. 18, xi. 8, 10; φύραμα, ix. 21. xi. 16.

In JC alone the following: ἐπικαλέω, x. 12, 13, 14; μαρτυρέω, iii. 21, x. 2; προτίθημι, i. 13, iii. 25; ῥῆμα, x. 8 bis, 17, 18; στηρίζω, i. 11, xvi. 25; διαστολή, iii. 22, x. 12; δικαίωσις, iv. 25, v. 18; and the phrase ὑπακοὴ πίστεως, i. 5, xvi. 26.

In CJ alone the following: ἀδύνατος, viii. 3, xv. 1; ἀλλότριος, xiv. 4, xv. 20; ἀπεκδέχομαι, viii. 19, 23, 25; ἀρέσκω, viii. 8, xv. 1, 2, 3; ἀσθένεια, vi. 19, viii. 26; διδασκαλία, xii. 7, xv. 4; δόκιμος, xiv. 18, xvi. 10; δουλόω, vi. 18, 22; ἐκκλησία, xvi. 1, 4, 5, 16, 23; ἐκλεκτός, viii. 33, xvi. 13; ἐλευθερόω, vi. 18, 21, viii. 2, 21;˷ ἕνεκα, viii. 36, xiv. 20; εὐάρεστος, xii. 1, 2, xiv. 18; θανατόω, vii. 4, viii. 13, 36; θνητός, vi. 12, viii. 11; καινότης, vi. 4, vii. 6; μηκέτι, vi. 6 xiv. 13, xv. 23; οἰκοδομή, xiv. 19, xv. 2; οὐδείς, xiv. 7 bis, 14, viii. 1; πάθημα, vii. 5, viii. 18; παράκλησις, xii. 8, xv. 4, 5; παρίστημι, vi. 13 bis, 16, 19 bis, xii. 1, xiv. 10, xvi. 2; προσλαμβάνω, xiv. 1, 3, xv. 7; φρόνημα,

4*

viii. 6 bis, 7, 27; χωρίζω, viii. 35, 39; κυριεύω, vi. 9, 14, vii. 1, xiv. 9.

b. It is to the same effect, when certain words are used predominantly, though not quite exclusively, in one of the four parts. Thus in G¹ we find τιμή 4 times, elsewhere only once; in G² γίνομαι 25 times, in G¹ twice, JC 3 times, in CJ 7 times, i. e., six times as often in G² as on the average in either of the three others — certainly a most remarkable phenomenon; ἐλεέω 7 times, elsewhere only once; θέλω 12 times, elsewhere thrice; σπέρμα 8 times, elsewhere once; καλέω 5 times, elsewhere only viii. 30, where it occurs twice; εὑρίσκω 4 times, elsewhere only once; in CJ ἕκαστος 4 times, elsewhere once; ἐλπίζω 3 times, elsewhere once; ζάω 18 times, elsewhere 4 times; κτίσις 5 times, elsewhere twice; πνεῦμα (of the Divine Spirit) 21 times, elsewhere 3 times; σῶμα 10 times, elsewhere 3 times; ἀποθνήσκω 17 times, elsewhere 6 times; ἀδελφός 14 times, elsewhere 6 times [1].

c. Again, we may notice that certain very common words are in some of the four parts wholly wanting. Thus, in G¹ we nowhere meet with ἅγιος, ἀκούω, ἁμαρτία, μᾶλλον, πάλιν, πατήρ, πίστις, πολύς, πῶς, χάρις. In G² we miss αἰώνιος, ἀλλήλος, ἁπαρτάνω, ἀπο-

---

[1] The argument would be still stronger, if we should follow the example of the analysts of the Pentateuch, and in all cases of such rare use of a word in any one of the parts should simply assume that they are instances of the working over which the sections have received from the hands of R. But our case is so strong that we do not need to make this assumption, though it might be more scientific to do so.

κάλυψις, δύναμαι, έκαστος, θέλημα, καρδία. JC nowhere uses ἀγαπάω, ἀδικία, δυνατός, έργον, κακός, καλέω, κρίνω, λογίζομαι, λόγος, νοῦς, ὅσος, πράσσω, σῶμα, φόβος, φρονέω. CJ never uses ἀλήθεια, δίκαιος, Ἕλλην, ἐχθρός, θέλω, Ἰουδαῖος, κόσμος, κρίμα, ὄνομα, ὀργή, πράσσω, σωτηρία.

d. It is still more significant of diversity of authorship, when for the same thought in the different parts different words are used. Thus we find for

Accuse	in	G¹ κατηγορέω, ii. 15; CJ ἐγκαλέω, viii. 33.
Be called	„	G¹ ἐπονομάζομαι, ii. 17; G² καλέομαι, ix. 26; CJ χρηματίζω, vii. 3.
Compassion	„	G² ἔλεος, ix. 23, xi. 31; CJ οἰκτιρμός, xii. 1.
Continually	„	G² διαπαντός, xi. 10; JC πάντοτε, i. 10.
Command	„	JC ἐπιταγή, xvi. 26; G¹, xiii. 9, and G², vii. 8, 9, 10, 11, 12, 13, ἐντολή.
Deliver (from sin)	„	G² ῥύομαι, vii. 24, xi. 26; CJ ἐλευθερόω, vi. 18, 22, viii. 2, 21.
Despise	„	G¹ καταφρονέω, ii. 4; CJ ἐξουθενέω, xiv. 3, 10.
Disobedience	„	G² ἀπείθεια, xi. 30, 32; JC παρακοή, v. 19.
Falsehood	„	G¹ ψεῦδος, i. 25; G² ψεῦσμα, iii. 7.
Foolish	„	JC ἀνόητος, i. 14; G¹ ἀσύνετος, i. 21, 31, and ἄφρων, ii. 20.
Goodness	„	CJ ἀγαθωσύνη, xv. 14; G¹, ii. 4, and G², iii. 12, xi. 22, χρηστότης.
Hardness of heart	„	G¹ σκληρότης, ii. 5; G² πώρωσις, xi. 25.

Hinder	in	JC κωλύω, i. 13; CJ ἐγκόπτω, xv. 22.
Kill	„	G¹ φονεύω, xiii. 9; G² ἀποκτείνω, vii. 11, xi. 3; CJ θανατόω, vii. 4, viii. 13, 36.
Likewise	„	G¹ ὁμοίως, i. 27; CJ ὡσαύτως, viii. 26.
Manifest	„	G¹ φανερός, i. 19, ii. 28; JC ἐμφανής, x. 20.
Obey	„	G¹ πείθω, ii. 8; JC, x. 16, and CJ, vi. 12, 16, 17, ὑπακούω.
On account of	„	CJ ἕνεκα, viii. 36, xiv. 20, and δία; in the others only δία.
Ordain	„	G¹ τάσσω, xiii. 1; JC ὁρίζω, i. 4.
Passion	„	G¹ πάθος, i. 26; CJ. πάθημα, vii. 5.
Persevere	„	G¹ προσκαρτερέω, xii. 12, xiii. 6; G² ἐπιμένω, xi. 22, 23.
Pray	„	JC δέομαι, i. 10; CJ προσεύχομαι, viii. 26.
Publish	„	G² διαγγέλλω, ix. 17; CJ, xv. 21, ἀναγγέλλω.
Recompense	„	G¹ ἀντιμισθία, i. 27; G² μισθός, iv. 4, and ἀνταπόδομα, xi. 9.
Rejoice	„	G¹ χαίρω, xii. 12, 15, xvi. 19; JC εὐφραίνω, xv. 10.
Send	„	JC ἀποστέλλω, x. 15; CJ πέμπω, viii. 3.
Speak as a man	„	G² κατὰ ἄνθρωπον λέγω, iii. 5; CJ ἀνθρώπινον λέγω, vi. 19.
Stand	„	CJ στήκω, xiv. 4; G², xi. 20, and JC, v. 2, ἵστημι.

Take pleasure	„ G¹ συνευδοκέω, i. 32; G² συνήδομαι vii. 22.
Understand	„ G¹ νοέω, i. 20; G², iii. 11, and CJ, xv. 21, συνίημι.
Walk (conduct one's self)	„ G² στοιχέω, iv. 12; G¹, xiii. 13, and CJ, vi. 4, viii. 4, xiv. 15, περιπατέω.
Weak	„ JC ἀσθενής, v. 6; CJ ἀδύνατος, xv. 1.
Where	„ CJ ὅπου, xv. 20; G², iv. 15, ix. 26, and JC, v. 20, οὗ.
Word (of God)	„ G² λόγος, iii. 4, ix. 6, 9; JC ῥῆμα, x. 8, 17.

e. Finally, we observe that *vice versa* the same word has in the different parts different meanings. Thus, ἀγαπάω and ἀγάπη are used by G¹ only in reference to the love of men to one another, xii. 9, xiii. 8, 9, 10; whereas G², ix. 13, 25, JC, v. 5, 8, and CJ, viii. 28, 35, 37, 39, xv. 30, use them exclusively (except in xiv. 15) of the love of God or of love to God. — As already pointed out, σάρξ has an ethico-religious sense only in CJ; and so its opposite πνεῦμα. — Likewise ψυχή is used by G¹, ii. 9, xiii. 1, as synonymous with "person"; by G², xi. 3, and CJ, xvi. 4, in the sense of "life". — Δικαίωμα is used by JC, v. 16, 18, in the sense of "justification"; by G¹, i. 32, ii. 26, and CJ, viii. 4, in the sense of "ordinance."

The foregoing observations respecting the vocabulary of the four writers are borne out when we examine the *style* of the several parts. G¹ is preeminently oratorical, G² argumentative, JC doctrinal, CJ emotional. Observe how in i. 18 — ii. 29 the writer draws out his picture in a rich fulness of description which nowhere else has a parallel. The direct appeal in ch. ii. is a fine specimen of rhetorical address, such as occurs in no other part of the Epistle. G² on the other hand delights in arguing a proposition which the reader is conceived to be disinclined to accept. Ch. iv. is devoted to an argument derived from Abraham's faith. Chh. ix. and xi. are nothing but debates with objectors, the objections being often put into the mouth of the reader (see ix. 14, 19, xi. 1, 19). JC is neither oratorical nor argumentative. He occupies himself chiefly in stating the doctrine of justification by faith. He introduces it, after getting through with his preface, at i. 16, 17, repeats it in a fuller form in iii. 21—26, and enlarges on it still more in v. 1—21. In all this there is no argument, and no appeal, but rather a dogmatic statement of the doctrine of salvation through Christ. In the remainder of what we have from JC we find, it is true, especially in ix. 1—5, an expression of feeling. But even here there is no direct appeal or address, and he at once passes (x. 1—21) to an unimpassioned statement of the conditions of salvation, and of the obstinacy of the Jews with reference to the gospel. Finally, in CJ we discern a still different style. In a certain sense we may say that he unites in himself all the features which we have severally ascribed to the other three. He is oratorical in viii. 31—39; he is argumentative in vi. 1—3, 15, 16; he is dogmatic in viii. 1—4. But through all this there runs a vein which makes CJ's style distinct from them all.

We have called it an emotional element. The subjects are treated of as if by one who is unfolding the treasures of a deep experience. He states his doctrine; but the point of it all is in the setting forth of the deliverance and the blessednes of which the Christian has been made partaker. He is eloquent, but it is eloquence which gushes up out of a sense of personal salvation. He can argue, but it is only for the sake of impressing on his readers the reality of the liberty and the security which they enjoy.

The difference between the four writers in respect of style may be otherwise stated as follows: G^1 is psychological; G^2 is historical; JC is didactic; CJ is hortatory. G^1 sets forth the workings of conscience, of sinful passion, of deceitful self-righteousness. G^2 illustrates his arguments from historical facts. JC labors to indoctrinate his readers by repetition and amplification. CJ even in his doctrinal part makes his practical aim obvious, and he follows it up with an extended series of exhortations (xii. 1—8, xiii. 14—xv. 7).

These are general statements which might be illustrated in detail. But it will suffice to have called attention to the salient points in the style of the several writers. The reader can verify our statements for himself.

Taking now all these various linguistic features together, and observing that they all point in the same direction; furthermore, bearing in mind that they confirm the previous argument from the contents of the Epistle, one can scarcely longer entertain a doubt that our main proposition is demonstrated.

The foregoing analysis had been elaborated even to its fullest details before the publication of Völter's treatise on the composition of the chief Pauline Epistles. Inasmuch as he undertakes a similar critical analysis, and also finds the Epistle to the Romans to have been the work of several authors, but comes to a decidedly different result from ours, it may seem as if such a difference in the result casts some discredit upon the whole effort to trace the composition of the Epistle by the critical method. But such a disagreement proves only that not both of the results can be correct. Whether Völter's analysis or that which we have presented is the correct one must be left to the reader's judgment.

Völter, though he regards all of the Epistle to the Galatians as spurious, strangely enough holds *some* of the Epistle to the Romans to be really Pauline, viz., i. 1ª, 7, 5, 6, 8—17; v. 1—12, 15—19, 21; vi. 1—13, 16—23; xii. 1—xiii. 14; xv. 14—32; xvi. 21—23. For this view he gives no better reason than that Steck's objections do not touch those parts of the Epistle which he holds to be genuine. What is stranger still, he assigns to Paul a large part of precisely those portions which we have shown to belong to the two latest writers, JC and CJ. Then, on the ground of certain differences in the conception and presentation of the topics, he enucleates six interpolators, among whom he distributes the rest of the Epistle. It would be strange if he had not in many particulars coincided with us in our division. Thus, he detaches vii. 7—25 from its connection and assigns it to the third interpolator. Also he separates iii. 21 *sqq.* from the foregoing, though he makes the section extend to iv. 25. Again, xv. 7—13 is recognised as not belonging where it is found, thus agreeing with us, except that verse 7 is unaccountably included in the section, though it manifestly belongs with the foregoing [1].

It is almost incredible that ch. vi. should be dissevered from ch. viii., and one reason given for the separation should be that the Christology is different, since in viii. 32 Christ is called God's own Son, and is conceived as pre-existent (p. 59). But Christ is called God's Son also in the Pauline part, v. 10. A similar infelicity occurs on p. 77, where the second interpolator is distinguished from Paul as making Jesus' resurrection the starting-point, whereas Paul makes Jesus' death the immediate object of faith — this, in the face of iii. 25, which he assigns to the interpolator! The treatise is full of similar fallacies; and the argument turns largely on subtle distinctions to maintain which single verses are arbitrarily ejected (e. g., vi. 14, 15). But we

---

[1] For the convenience of those who may not have access to Völter's work, we may here give the results of his analysis. After eliminating the above mentioned parts ascribed to Paul, the remainder is divided as follows: (1) i. 1b—4; i. 18—ii. 13; ii. 16—iii. 20; viii. 1, 3—39. (2) iii. 21—iv. 25; v. 13, 14, 20; vi. 14, 15; vii. 1—6; ix. 1—x. 21; xiv. 1—xv. 6. (3) vii. 7—25; viii. 2. (4) xi. 1—36; xv. 7—13. (5) ii. 14, 15. (6) xvi. 1—20, 24, 25—27.

cannot undertake to criticise the work in detail, being assured that the best refutation of it will be a candid examination of the preceding analysis.

Having now presented the dogmatic and the linguistic arguments, it remains to consider the historical argument. First, however, we may fortify the ground already gained by a comparison of our work with that which has been done in Old Testament criticism. Our analysis, being wholly in accordance with the most approved critical methods, confirms, and is confirmed by, the results of criticism in other connections. Particularly it is interesting to notice how here, as in the case of the Pentateuch, a diversity in the use of the divine names (reckoning the names of the Redeemer among them) was the first clew which suggested the analysis, while here as there this clew led to the discovery of other more fundamental differences, viz., those which characterise the general cast of doctrinal thought, and finally these two coincident indications are found to be confirmed by the general linguistic peculiarities of the several sections.

In some respects our analysis may be pronounced even more thoroughly grounded than that of the Pentateuch. For there the distinction in the use of the divine names prevails only through Genesis and a small part of Exodus; afterwards other criteria have to be depended on. In Romans, however, the criterion can be applied throughout the entire book. Moreover, when we consider the differences of doctrinal type, the distinction between G^1, G^2, JC, and CJ is so clear and radical that it is obvious to every one as soon as it is once detected and stated. The ethico-legal position of G^1 cannot be mistaken for the mystical one of CJ. G^2's doctrine of faith in God's sovereign decree is very different from JC's doctrine of faith in Christ's atoning death. These differences, be it noticed, appear in the treatment of the same general theme; they run deep; and they are clearly marked. The distinctions between the doctrines of the different writers of the Pentateuch, however, are by no means so important and are not always clearly made out at all. That this is the case is natural enough, to be sure, considering the general subject of which the Pentateuch treats. But our comparison holds. For example, when the two narrators of the flood are distinguished, the distinction is not one that can be verified by the adducing of differences in the general point of view or in the conception of the facts. To be sure, P (Gen. vi. 19) makes Noah bring in *two* of every kind of animals, while J (vii. 2, 3) makes him bring in *seven* pairs of the clean animals; but otherwise there is no clearly-defined difference between P and J in their representation of facts or their conception of God. And even the distinction respecting the animals is somewhat confused by the fact that in vii. 7—9 is an account which appears to be Elohistic, and yet apparently tries to blend the Elohistic description (vi. 19, 20) with the Jehovistic (vii. 2, 3), and has therefore to be assigned to the Redactor. Similarly in disentangling the three writers from whom the account of the Egyptian plagues has been compiled it is difficult to find any criteria that are so marked and uniformly found as to make unmistakable the source of the several parts. Captious objectors [1], therefore, can often seem to throw considerable discredit on the analysis, impregnable as it must appear to all open and candid minds.

So again, as regards the chronological order of the several parts, our hypothesis respecting the Epistle to the Romans must command unhesitating assent even from those who might question the results of the latest criticism of the Old Testament. It hardly needs an argument to prove that G^1 must have written before G^2. He represents simply reformed Judaism, emphasising the duty of keeping the law, but meaning thereby the moral law rather than the ceremonial. G^2, who tells of a justification that is to be secured apart from the law, must represent a later phase of Jewish-Christian thinking. Men had begun to find out that the law could not practically be obeyed in its strictness; and they looked for some method of relief, and found it in a divine act of justification conditioned on faith in God. This faith could not at first have had Jesus, a mere man, for its object; and consequently JC, who agrees with G^2 in emphasising the importance of faith, but

---

[1] Like Prof. W. H. Green, *Pentateuch Analysis* (in *Essays on Pentateuchal Criticism by various Writers*, New York 1888). It may be added to the foregoing considerations, that in our analysis of Romans there is much less of minute chopping up of the text into small parts than in the analysis of the Pentateuch. And we do not find it necessary to make so much use of R in accounting for phenomena that make against our hypothesis.

makes the atoning Christ the object of that faith, must have come still later, when Jesus had begun to receive divine honours. And CJ, with his mystical notion of spiritual union between Christ and the Christian — a conception in which the Old Testament notion of sacrifice (still found, though idealised, in JC) is completely lost — marks a still later form of the development of Christian doctrine. No intelligent man could seriously think of changing this order. It is deduced from what obviously must have been the natural process of evolution.

The current view of critics respecting the chronological order of the Old Testament books also has regard to what the natural process of evolution must have been. The analysis, it is true, may be insisted on as indisputably correct, even down to Wellhausen's J^1, J^2, J^3, Q^1, Q^2, Q^3, etc. But it may still be argued that possibly the authors wrote in a different order from that which is now commonly assumed. The present theory respecting the order differs widely from that which prevailed at first; and among those who accept the critical partition there are still very many who contend that P cannot have been so late a development as Wellhausen and others suppose. It is at least not self-evident that the Levitical ritual must have been the latest outcome of the religious history of the nation. The apparent contempt for all ceremonial religion expressed by Jeremiah and the Second Isaiah would hardly seem to be a natural precursor of the introduction of a ceremonial system so elaborate as that of the Priestly Code. To be sure, there comes in here the evidence of history and the ritual proclivities of the Books of Chronicles, to confirm the theory that formalism did follow rather than precede the prophetic period. The books of Judges, Samuel, and Kings, it would seem, make it clear that before the Exile little or nothing was known of the Levitical Code. The books of Chronicles, written about 300 B. C., evidently try to reconstruct history so as to make it conform to the newly issued Priestly Code. Consequently the order of development assumed in the now dominant hypothesis may seem to be proved to be the actual one.

But what after all hinders any one from putting the dates of the books of Judges, Samuel, and Kings even later than 300 B. C., and so making them, rather than the Chronicles, the last product of the religious evolution? The mere fact that those books do not bring history down so far as the Chronicles do, proves of course nothing; for we can assume that these books (as it is commonly assumed that the Chronicles) were written for the very purpose of reconstructing history. In that case we should have to assume that the author deliberately endeavoured to make the impression of being an older writer than the author of the Chronicles, and wrote for the purpose of representing the Israelites from the time of Joshua on to have been much less ritualistic than the Chronicles had pictured them.

Should it be objected that the prophetic books, belonging to the very centre of the period in question, agree for substance with Samuel and Kings rather than with Chronicles, the answer is near at hand. What is the evidence that the prophetical books are not also the product of the latest period of the development? May not the same school of writers from which emanated the books of Samuel and Kings have also written the prophetical books? Of many of the prophets we know absolutely nothing but that certain writings are ascribed to them. Tradition may have preserved the names of some; and they themselves having left no writings, these reformers of the post-exilic period may have produced writings in the form of prophecies and ascribed them to this or that one of the old prophets; in other cases they may have invented both the name and the writings.

No one can find any difficulty with this hypothesis on the ground that writers of so late a period could not have so well simulated the appearance of having written four or five hundred years earlier. Every one knows that the Hexateuch was composed an equal length of time after the date at which it purports to have been produced; and yet it is indisputable, as the orthodox apologists are not slow to point out, that the authors succeeded marvellously in giving the work the colouring of the period just following the exodus. Nor can there be any moral scruple in the one case more than in the other. And the upshot is simply that all the Old Testament, instead of a large part of it, is thus made to be substantially a fiction. Of course a thread of historical truth runs through it. The list of kings, and many historical events, may have been derived from a fairly trustworthy tradition. That this is the case is shown by the confirmatory records of Assyria recently unearthed. But in so far as the books have a *religious* character, what is to hinder one's making them all the product of pious fiction? The poetical books are such at any rate, unless we except some of the Psalms; and certainly the most of these are fictitiously ascribed to David and others who did not write them. Criticism has discovered that the most or all of them were written during the Maccabean period or after. Thus we have the great advantage that no sharp line of distinction can be drawn between two classes of books — the genuine and the spurious. All are made to stand on the same plane, and all therefore can be judged on their own merits. The most recent criticism has reached this result as regards the New Testament. And there is an obvious advantage, as Steck[1] forcibly observes, in not having a Bible made up in part of genuine, and in part of spurious, books. In such a case, he says, the latter are at a disadvantage as compared with the others, whereas if it is once recognised to have been the way of those times to write pseudonymously and fictitiously, all unpleasant impressions are removed; all the books are alike worthy of honour. At present, however, Old Testament criticism stands about where the Tübingen school stood as regards the New Testament. A part of the Testament is accepted as substantially authentic and genuine, in order by means of it to prove the spuriousness and untrustworthiness of the rest. It

---

[1] *Der Galaterbrief*, p. 385.

being assumed that Judges, Samuel, and Kings can be depended on as for substance genuine history, and that the prophetical writings for the most part were produced at the time claimed for them, these books are made the touchstone for testing the value of all the others. This has been done without any thorough critical examination of the books assumed to be genuine, just as Baur and his school accepted the first four Pauline Epistles as undoubtedly genuine without any serious effort to sift the question of their genuineness.

The most recent criticism[1], however, is showing that the conflict between the Judaistic and Pauline parties, though real, reached its culmination a century after Paul's time, that Paul himself was not so obnoxious to Jewish Christians as has been supposed, and that therefore the so-called Pauline Epistles are all to be referred to the second century. Just so it may be argued that the conflict between ritualism and a freer religion in the Old Covenant did not reach its climax till some time after the captivity, and that then there sprang up a series of books on each side[2]. On the side of the ritualistic

---

[1] See Steck, *Der Galaterbrief*, pp. 371—382.

[2] Substantially this view of the late origin of all the historical and prophetical books has been advanced by certain French critics. E. g. Ernest Havet, *Le Christianisme et ses Origines*, Tom 3, Préface, p. vii., says that, so far from needing to assume the genuineness of the prophetical books, "one can with more plausibility suppose that they had their origin in the contest of the Jews with the kings of Syria in the second century before our era". Similarly Maurice Vernes, *Une nouvelle hypothèse sur la com-*

party there were produced the legislative books of Exodus, Leviticus, and Numbers (at least the bulk of what now constitutes those books), the historical books of Joshua, Chronicles, Ezra, Nehemiah, and Esther, and the prophetical books of Haggai, the first part of Zechariah, Malachi, and the latter part of Ezekiel. On the side of the more liberal party there were produced the historical books of Genesis, Deutoronomy, Judges, Ruth, Samuel, and Kings, and the larger part of the prophetical and poetical books. Then of course there was a mediating party; and to this party may be ascribed the intermingling of opposite elements in many of the books, as in Exodus, Deutoronomy, Joshua, Ezekiel, and to some extent in the Psalms (cf., e. g., Ps. li. 16, 17 with verses 18, 19) and Jeremiah (e. g., vii. 21—26 cannot have come from the same author as xvii. 26). Now as in the history of the Christian Church the freer, or Pauline, party ultimately gained the upper hand, so it may be presumed that in the Jewish Church the more liberal, or at least the mediating, party finally gained the ascendency. But the most natural order would be first the reign of formalism, next the reaction in favor of freedom. And accordingly it may be argued that the now prevalent view as to the order of the production of the Old Testament books needs a revision.

But it may be said that this mixing together of the different and even contradictory productions

---

position et l'origine du Deutéronome. 1887. L. Horst, *Études sur le Deutéronome* in the *Revue de l'histoire des religions.* 1888.

of Old Testament piety cannot easily be accounted for, provided they sprang up so nearly together. One would suppose that they must, from the necessity of the case, by the mutual hostility of the parties, have been kept distinct. But such an objection overlooks the peculiarity of the religious mind of those times. All writings which appeared laying claim to the character of inspired, prophetic, authoritative Scriptures were accepted as such, whatever may have been their particular religious drift. They were put side by side, or even intermingled with one another, and the contradictions apparently not recognised except by those who wrote them. Evidently the Jews of Christ's time had no conception of the self-contradictory character of their sacred books; and as little did the Christians in general of the times of Irenaeus and Origen have any conception of the essential irreconcilableness of the different books of the New Testament. Nothing, therefore, was easier than to introduce a new book into the list of authoritative writings.

It may possibly be objected to this suggestion of ours respecting the date of the historic and prophetical books, that the Greek translation of the Old Testament was begun at least as early as 250 B. C., and that therefore it is hardly conceivable that between 300 (the date of the Chronicles) and the beginning of this translation these books of the freer party could have sprung up. But it is not necessary to suppose that all of them originated in this short time. The conflict must have been longer than this. Nothing hinders our supposing that Genesis, for instance, was written not long after the introduction of the Levitical Code, and with it the Jehovistic parts of Exodus. On either side piece by piece the legislation and the history came out, the liberal party always matching the works of the formalists with something designed to counteract their influence, the books of Chronicles being at last followed by Samuel and Kings. No one knows when the translation was completed. But it is not at all necessary to assume that a long time must have intervened between the production and the reception of the books. Being set forth as ancient and divinely inspired documents, they were almost immediately accepted as such. Any one who can believe (as nearly all the critics do believe) that the book of Deutoronomy could have been acknowledged as of divine authority as soon as it was promulgated, though it had only just been gotten up by the prophetical party, can find no difficulty in supposing that all the other books had a similar origin and a similar prompt recognition.

But, it may be said, this very book of Deutoronomy is the one which the critics declare to have been "found", i. e., composed, in the reign of Josiah, and that therefore this book at least must have been older than the time of the exile. But the objector forgets that this story about the finding of the book occurs in a history which we now assume to have been composed about 275 B. C., and which is for the most part a fictitious history. This story about the finding of the law is one of the fictions. That the book referred to was our present book of Deutoronomy is a mere assumption. Whether the author of the story meant it to refer to that book or to something else, no one can tell, and it is useless to discuss the question, so long as we regard the story itself as apocryphal [1].

But this is somewhat of a digression; and it also to some extent anticipates what more properly comes into our next chapter, where we must consider some questions relating to historical evidence.

---

[1] Inasmuch as the same story is found also in the Chronicles, our hypothesis requires us to suppose that the author of Kings borrowed the story from the Chronicles. The fact that it is found in both books, while yet both authors cannot be supposed to have had Deutoronomy in mind (the Chronicler of course meaning his readers to suppose the found book to be the Levitical code), shows how futile it is to speculate on that point.

CHAPTER IV.

THE HISTORICAL ARGUMENT.

Historical facts are often set over against the results of critical inspection, and the conclusion is drawn that the actual must rule out the hypothetical, when they are in conflict. Of course. But we must take pains to form clear conceptions as to what the antithesis of actual and theoretical really amounts to. If it should be affirmed that the foregoing argumentation is a mere hypothesis, or even a capricious conceit, in support of which no discoverable historical fact can be adduced, we answer: This despised argumentation consists in the presentation of *facts* — the *fact* that the Epistle to the Romans evidently contains four distinct types of doctrine, and the *fact* that the linguistic characteristics of the Epistle correspond to this fourfold division. These facts constitute the basis of the argument. If now it is affirmed that it is after all not demonstrated that four different men were concerned in the production of the book, we can only rejoin that such a method of reasoning, logically carried out, would put an end to all scientific judgments. For instance what is *geology* but a combination of theories on the basis of certain observed facts? The *science* comes from the application of theory to fact. So long as we stop with the bare isolated facts, we have no science. So with chemistry. Men observe certain changes, the effect of certain combinations, and by degrees come to make hypotheses concerning various atoms, or invisible particles, which are assumed to lie at the basis of the observed phenomena. Just so in the examination of a book. A book is not scientifically understood, when one has merely seen the forms of the letters, or has learned to pronounce the words, or even to make out the meaning of the individual sentences. One must look at the book in its connection, must discover the leading thought and general aim of the book, must penetrate into the spirit and intent of the author, and get an insight into the history of the origin of the book, before one can be said to have understood it scientifically. If now our theory of the Epistle to the Romans does not correspond to known facts or fails to account for them; if, rather, a different theory enables one to get a more scientific knowledge of the Epistle, very well. In both cases, however, we begin with acknowledged facts, and in both cases we end with a — hypothesis.

What then is meant when men talk of the historical arguments which are supposed to be so fatal to our theory? Primarily, no doubt, they have in mind the traditional reports concerning the early history of the Christian Church; and they imagine that these reports make the Pauline authorship of the Epistle certain — so certain that no critical insight can be competent to overthrow it. What is to be said to this? Simply that these supposed facts of history, like all others, must be examined, in order to determine what really is actual in them. In other words, criticism must deal with the alleged historic facts as well as with the book. In both cases we must first ask, what is the fact? and next, what is the explanation and meaning of it?

Moreover, we should remember that it is easier to find out what is actual in the book in question than to find out the exact truth of the history in question. The book is before us, and has definite, unmistakable traits. The historical testimonies concerning the authorship of it are much less definite and unambiguous. Every thing depends on when and by whom the testimonies were written. This must first be investigated before we can attach any weight to them. But it is no trifling work to penetrate through two thousand years in order to test the value of these alleged testimonies. It cannot be simply taken for granted that the alleged witnesses are the real witnesses, or that they are as old as commonly supposed. If we are told that tradition vouches for the genuineness of the testimonies, we can only answer that the origin and worth of this tradition must be critically examined before we can accept it as authoritative. And in this examination criticism must make use of its own insight and its hypotheses, precisely as it must with the Epistle to the Romans itself.

No doubt, tradition affirms the Pauline authorship of the Epistle in question. But no less has tradition affirmed the Mosaic authorship of the Pentateuch and the Johannean authorship of the Fourth Gospel. But *what vouches for the tradition?* It, too, must ultimately submit to critical inspection and critical judgment.

When, now, we consider the Epistle to the Romans in the light of the historical questions connected with it, we may in the first place claim that our conception of it, instead of being in conflict with history, is particularly fitted to solve the historical problems which have beset the traditional view. For example, whole libraries have been produced in the effort to settle the question, whether the Epistle was written to a Jewish-Christian, or a Gentile-Christian, church. And really, as the Epistle reads, it is no easy matter to answer the question; for both views are favoured by it. In other words, the several writers had different readers in mind when they wrote. G^1 and G^2 seem to have been Jewish Christians, and wrote for readers of the same class, as may be seen from such passages as ii. 17, 24—29, iv. 1. It is true, G^2 apparently had a mixed congregation in mind; ix. 22—24 sounds even as if the readers were regarded as converts from heathenism. But a closer examination shows that when the writer says, "us, whom he also called, not from the Jews only, but also from the Gentiles", he regards the readers as preponderantly Jewish

Christians. The same is to be said of xi. 13, where G² does not mean to imply that his readers are all Gentiles, but rather, because the most of them are not such, he singles out the Gentile part particularly, and says, "I speak to [those of] you who are Gentiles". True, he emphasises the fact that the Jews in general have rejected the gospel; but this does not indicate that the church addressed did not consist mostly of Christian Jews.

JC, on the other hand, regards his readers as chiefly Gentiles. This must be the impression which he makes on every one who reads this part alone, and is not fettered by the notion that the Epistle was all written by one man. When, therefore, Mangold[1] argues, with great ability and ingenuity, that Rom. i. 6, 13, 15 can be so interpreted as not to imply that the readers are conceived as mostly Gentile Christians, every one must see that he is contending against the obvious meaning of the passages. From his point of view he is doubtless correct. If the Epistle was written by one man, these passages may most naturally have to be interpreted in accordance with others which clearly point to Jewish Christians as the readers. But when we take JC alone, we find no clear indication that he is addressing himself particularly to Jewish Christians. He takes for granted, of course, that his readers are acquainted with Jewish history and the relation of Judaism to Christianity. Assuming the

---

[1] *Der Römerbrief und seine geschichtlichen Voraussetzungen*, 1884, p. 165, *sqq.*

name of Paul, he calls the Jews his "brethren" (ix, 3), and discourses at length concerning the attitude taken by the Jews towards the gospel. At x. 1 the "brethren" whom he addresses are different from the Jews about whom he is speaking. If one should object that just so G^2 at xi. 25, when he addresses his readers as "brethren", must regard them as Gentiles, we must remember, what was observed above, that he is now expressly addressing the Gentile minority of his readers (xi. 13).

As to CJ the case is somewhat different. For the most part, he says nothing which indicates whether his readers are conceived to be Jews or Gentiles. But the passage on which Mangold particularly relies (vii. 4—6) for the proof of his view is found in CJ; and it may be that in this passage there is reference to the Mosaic law. What he says in vi. 14, 15, inasmuch as νόμος is without the article, may be understood generally. And in vii. 1 νόμος is anarthrous also; and it is possible to assume that, when he afterwards uses the article, he has in mind "the law" in its wider aspect. But this question may be left unsettled.

The main point here urged is that according to our view of the case this whole contention about the nationality of the readers of the Epistle is set aside. The truth is, we do not know to whom any part of the letter was written, or whether, strictly speaking, the several parts were ever sent to anybody. They were simply written by men who wished them to be regarded as letters that had been addressed to somebody. Evidently, then, these documents throw no light on the question, what the original Roman church was fifty or a hundred years before these writings were produced; and it is therefore idle to attempt to harmonize the several parts of the letter in order to settle a question which can be settled only by genuine historical documents, not by pseudonymic inventions.

Just so with reference to the much debated point, why Paul, who had never seen the Romans, should have addressed to them his most elaborate letter. When once we have come to see that Paul never wrote this letter, and probably never wrote any, the question is answered; and there is no further need of solving a mystery which does not exist.

Our view disposes of several other questions concerning which learned scholars have beat their brains. For example, the question, when and where Paul wrote this and other letters; the question, whether the utterances of the letters can be reconciled with those of the Acts; the question, how the doctrines of the several letters are to be reconciled with one another, etc., etc. It is obvious that these are all factitious difficulties. If Paul never wrote any letters at all, we are relieved of the task of deciding when and why and where he wrote them; and quite as little do we need to harmonize the doctrines of one of the letters with those of the others. It is clear that this is a great simplification of the problem of the historical inquirer.

Still certain questions will press upon some minds, and we must attend to them.

1. Why may we not assume that at least *one*

of the four writers of the so-called Epistle to the Romans was really Paul? Of course four different men could not each have been the Apostle; but one of them might have been.

This is certainly an admissible question. But which of the four shall we select? One might at first blush think of JC; for he alone expressly calls himself Paul. But manifestly this proves nothing, if the writing is pseudonymous, especially as G^2 and CJ also, though they do not use the name, yet evidently wish to be thought to be the Apostle (cf. xi. 1, xv. 22—32, xvi. 1 *sqq*.) And if the omitted introductions were extant, we should probably find that all four of the writers (at least these three) call themselves Paul. In G^1 alone, as his part of the Epistle has been preserved, do we fail to find something which appears to involve a claim of Pauline authorship.

Yet G^1 is the very one, if any one of the four, who must be called Paul the Apostle. For, as we have shown, he must have been the earliest of the four writers; and no one supposes him to have written before the time of Paul. As we have made it clear that by far the greater part of the Epistle is not Pauline, and that this greater part contains just what is now-a-days called Paulinism, whereas G^1's doctrine is just the opposite, probably few can be found who will care to identify G^1 with the great Apostle. But even G^1's doctrine is probably more developed than that of Paul himself could have been. If it is true, as it may be, that Paul was originally a zealous Pharisee, then as a Christian he can have been only a modified Pharisee, since all sudden and radical changes are contrary to the laws of evolution. His conversion, therefore, could have consisted only in his recognising Jesus as an estimable teacher of the law and in his learning to attach less weight to the outward form, and more to the inward essence, of the law.

It is true that even many of the more advanced critics have undertaken to show how Paul could have turned a complete theological somerset. But we cannot allow ourselves to be swayed by the inconsistencies of even the greatest scholars. Those who champion the regularity of the course of nature and reject all miracles, all sudden metamorphoses, no matter how well attested, cut but a sorry figure when they undertake to set forth how Saul of Tarsus may all of a sudden have been transformed from an ardent defender of the law into an open enemy of it[1]. If they had not supposed that the so-called Pauline Epistles were really genuine, and that therefore they must somehow adjust inconsistent things to one another, they would never have belied their own principles in this way. We have got beyond

---

[1] Examples of these efforts may be seen in Pfleiderer's *Urchristenthum*, pp. 32—43, and Hausrath's article on *Paulus* in Schenkel's *Bibellexicon*. In his earlier work, *Der Apostel Paulus*, Hausrath was disposed to throw aside the narrative of Paul's conversion as found in Acts, and undertook to account for the conversion in a psychological way without any vision. Pfleiderer's aim is to show that not the vision led to the conversion (as the N. T. represents), but that the conversion led to the vision. But if thus the whole point of the Biblical narrative can be so summarily set aside, why believe in any kind of vision at all?

all this, and are able to consider the question impartially. And an impartial view of the matter must lead us to affirm that not only not the greater part, but no part, of the Epistle to the Romans was written by Paul.

2. But we shall probably continue to hear the changes rung on the old allegation that from the earliest times on there never has been any doubt of the Pauline authorship of this Epistle. And we shall be told, too, that these Epistles, especially those to the Corinthians and the Galatians, bear the marks of genuineness in themselves, that one cannot but detect in them the utterances of a single person, that the allusions to the history and circumstances of Paul's time are so numerous, so natural, so manifestly unfictitious, and the coincidences between them and the narratives in the Acts so occult and yet so striking when brought out, that it is quite inconceivable that this could all have been composed a century after Paul's time.

Well, this sounds plausible enough. And indeed it is questionable whether such a feat could now be performed. The times are changed. On the one hand the writers of two thousand years ago seem to have been more able and skilful in literary fiction than those of the present day; and on the other hand the people seem then to have been more easily deceived than now. Of this the Gospels present a striking example. Every intelligent man knows that the account of Jesus' character and life which we there find must have been fictitious. We have there the picture of an entirely unique person, combining in himself human and divine qualities, His life and career are likewise unique. The miraculous runs through the whole and seems to be an essential part of it. The various and even opposite traits in the picture so blend together and seem to be so in harmony with one another that one believes almost in spite of himself that the history must have been an actual one. When we consider that four different narrators (in reality doubtless many more than four), in spite of important discrepancies in matters of detail, yet leave on us the impression that they are discoursing of a real and altogether extraordinary person, we cannot but be astonished at the ability and skill with which the description has been executed. The best proof of this ability and skill of the writers and redactors who have produced the evangelical narrative is the simple fact that the history has been believed so long and so widely. Nevertheless, since it is certain that, according to the established principles of modern science, miracles are a nonentity, and that such a supernatural and extraordinary person as the Jesus of the Gospels never could have existed, we must simply insist that the evangelical story is the product of a creative fancy. If now this ca be affirmed respecting this greater matter, all the easier is it to be believed that the Pauline Epistles may have been written by different authors, and that they nevertheless have all this while passed for Paul's genuine productions.

But the ancient testimonies — what about them? There has been, it is said, an unbroken tradition that Paul wrote these letters. But what of that? That a story, when once believed, should then be handed down, is a matter of course. The transmission of it, however, is not the same as an authentication of it. The vital question is, whether the original belief was well grounded. What now is the fact concerning the Epistle to the Romans? The first writer of whom we know that he quotes this Epistle is Irenaeus, who died about 190 A. D. In his writings the Pauline Epistles are frequently referred to and cited. If then Irenaeus's writings are themselves genuine (which we do not care to deny, but are not necessarily bound to take for granted), it is plain that Irenaeus not far from 175 A. D. acknowledged our thirteen Epistles as genuine works of Paul. We may admit this quite readily. For according to our own view the Epistle to the Romans was then extant in its present composite form. If G^1 wrote, say, between 80 und 90, G^2 between 100 and 110, JC between 115 and 125, and CJ between 130 and 140, what is there to hinder our supposing that Irenaeus regarded the composite Epistle as a genuine letter of Paul to the Romans? We need only to assume that the Redactor had brought the writings together, say, as early as 150 A. D., so that Irenaeus had the work before him years before he wrote his treatises.

It is true that certain passages from the First Epistle of Clement to the Corinthians are adduced as evidence that he was acquainted with our Epistle. And Clement is supposed to have written it about 96 A. D. What shall be said of this? In the first place, the passages in question are not quotations at all. Clement makes no mention of our Epistle. The passages merely resemble certain passages in the Epistle to the Romans. The resemblances are such as might occur without any acquaintance on the part of Clement with the Epistle in question. Both of them sprang up in the Christian Church, and breathed a common spirit. Many expressions of Christian doctrine might well have become almost stereotyped by repetition, so that it would be strange if we did not find in one writer what may sound like echoes of the other[1]. But, in the second place, we do not certainly know who wrote this Epistle to the Corinthians, nor when it was written. The letter does not itself profess to be Clement's, but only a letter from the church at Rome. Nothing but a tradition ascribes it to Clement. And the date of the letter is disputed, some putting it as late as 150 A. D. But thirdly, even if it should be conceded that the resemblances in question do betoken a dependence of one writer on the other, the dependence may as well be on the side of the Pseudo-Paul as on the side of Clement. It is a clear case of *petitio principii* when one reasons

---

[1] This cannot be said with the same positiveness of the references in Clement's Epistle to Paul's Epistles to the Corinthians, especially the passage (Ch. xlvii.) where Paul and his Epistle are expressly mentioned, and the Cephas and Apollos parties are alluded to. As to this, if the date of the Clement letter is put as late as some are inclined to do, the passage need not disturb us; if not, we need only to assume that the passage is an interpolation.

otherwise. It is in effect taken for granted that the Epistle to the Romans was written first, and then, because it is used in the Clement letter, it is inferred that it must have been written first! The same may be said of the alleged use of our Epistle in the Epistle of Polycarp, the Epistles of Ignatius, and other early Christian writings. As for Marcion, we get our knowledge of him from others. According to them he received ten of the Pauline Epistles as genuine, but expurgated them to suit his own views. How far these statements can be trusted, need not here be discussed; for it does not materially affect our conclusion. According to the latest authorities Marcion was in Rome somewhere between 140 and 170 A. D.; and the development of his Gnosticism and his doctrine of the New Testament may be dated any where within these years. Practically, therefore, he ranks with Irenaeus in point of time, as a witness respecting the New Testament Canon, only that we have Irenaeus's own writings, and have not Marcion's. At the best his testimony only shows, what we may admit, that by 160 or 170 A. D. a number of Epistles professing to be Pauline were accepted as such by Marcion, Irenaeus, and probably by the leading men of the Church generally. The testimony of the Muratorian Canon is to the same effect. But this takes us no farther back than the times of Irenaeus. We have then no trustworthy historical testimony which proves the Epistle to the Romans to have been known or received as Pauline before the middle of the second century.

3. But the objection will at once be raised, that

these testimonies of the second half of the second century in reality do more than to prove that the so-called Pauline Epistles were then extant. If they were at that time generally received as canonical Scriptures, it may be argued that this implies that they must have been known a long time before, else they could not at the time spoken of have acquired canonical authority. How is it conceivable, one may ask, that, if up to the middle of the century there were no Epistles of Paul known and reverenced in the Church, a whole series of such Epistles could make their appearance and become almost immediately accepted as genuine? Can it be supposed that the whole Church could be so easily persuaded that letters of Paul never before heard of had just been discovered? Would not all men of discretion at once have suspected a forgery? Is it, therefore, not necessary to suppose that the testimony of Irenaeus and his contemporaries really puts the origin of the Epistles very far back of Irenaeus's own time? Moreover, since Irenaeus was born possibly as early as 115 A. D., and lived in Rome about the middle of the second century, must he not have known that the Roman church had never had any letter from Paul? When the alleged letter appeared, must he not have known that it could be nothing but a fraudulent production? Furthermore, since Irenaeus was personally aquainted with Polycarp and others whose lives reached back far into the first century, and some of whom even had seen the apostles, must not Irenaeus have been certain that no letters of Paul were in existence, if in fact

Paul really had written none? How then could he in his later years speak of the Pauline Epistles as if there were no doubt whatever of their having been written by Paul?

These are certainly weighty considerations and must be met. Professor Steck[1] does not shut his eye to them; and we cannot do better than to adopt his treatment of the difficulty. He says: "When, as is generally done, one imagines that spurious apostolic writings could not come to be regarded as apostolic except by a gradual process and after a long series of years, at a time, say, when all information about their origin had been lost, and a different conception concerning them had gradually sprung up, the process is differently conceived from what it really must have been. We must not forget that such writings as the New Testament Epistles from the very beginning, and by their very address expressly claimed to have been written by the Apostle whose name they bear. They were deliberate forgeries, undertaken, in the spirit of that age and of all the literature of the early Church, by those who thought they were thereby serving the cause of Christian truth and of the Church. If the undertaking was successful, it is not necessary to assume a long time during which belief in their genuineness could be developed; this must have come about at once in those circles to whom the general drift of the new literary productions was welcome; whereas those of a different turn of mind expressed their opposition by

---

[1] *Der Galaterbrief*, p. 349 sq.

rejecting them. With the victory of the orthodox-ecclesiastical party the opinion that the writings were of apostolic origin became victorious also; and the opposition came by degrees to be regarded as the position of a heretical party. Therefore it is not at all necessary to assume a long obscure period of preparation for the appearance of such writings; rather, the fact doubless is, as Renan has somewhere said. that the traces of the appearance of such a writing in ecclesiastical literature generally indicate pretty exactly the time of its production."

Nothing could be more luminous and satisfactory than this exposition of the case. It puts the process so graphically before us that we seem to see it going on, and can hardly doubt the explanation more than the evidence of our senses. The process, then. was a very simple one — a simple, intentional, and successful deception. If those who produced and introduced the pseudepigraphic writings succeeded in persuading the Christian public, or a considerable part of it, that the forged writings were genuine, then the pious end was gained. The Epistle to the Romans, for example, was put together in the manner we have described and put out as an Epistle of Paul. The orthodox Christians were ready to accept it at once for what it professed to be, even without any evidence of a historical sort that such a letter had ever been heard of before. But why did it not seem strange to them that a letter of Paul's should thus suddenly turn up so long after the Apostle's death? Simply because "the drift of the new literary productions was welcome". The letter contained what men liked; and they believed that Paul had written it simply because they wanted to believe it. Those on the other hand who did not like the contents of the letter rejected it and called it spurious. On both sides the judgment was purely subjective. No one thought of instituting a historical investigation into the origin of the letter. Because the letter pleased the orthodox majority, it was orthodox to call it Pauline, and heretical to call it otherwise. And so it was with the whole New Testament. No book in it is genuine. But, as Steck elsewhere[1] forcibly observes, "If every thing is spurious, then nothing is 'spurious' any longer. The whole question comes to an end; there is no further quarrel about the genuineness or spuriousness of the New Testament books, but rather we try to understand each one by looking at its contents, and to assign it its place in the history of primeval Christianity accordingly. The moral scruple which used to make the critical positions distasteful to the Christian feeling disappears. We use and enjoy these writings now without any illusion, but also without prejudice, and do justice to their intrinsic worth".

Thus it appears that it required little time or effort to bring the New Testament into existence. That age was, as every one knows, a pseudepigraphical age. The world was full of pseudonymous writings. That was the fashion. And we owe to this fashion the fact that we have any New Testa-

---

[1] *L. c.* p. 385.

ment at all. For since neither Christ nor the first Christians wrote books, and the Church nevertheless was unwilling to adopt anything as canonical unless it was supposed to be apostolic, there was evidently no way in which a canon could be formed except by resort to this device of a pious fraud. Those who practised it thought, as Steck aptly says, that by this deception they were furthering the cause of Christian truth. Of course no conscientious objection could be urged against the procedure by any one possessed of a healthy conscience. If any one had been so morbid or whimsical as to object to it, the perpetrator would have only needed to reply in the crushing words of G^2, "If the truth of God through my lie abounded unto his glory, why am I also still judged as a sinner?" (Rom. iii. 7).

To be sure, one may say that, in spite of the pseudepigraphic mania of those times many genuine writings appeared and have been preserved down to our time. We have the works of Plato, Aeschylus, Horace, Seneca, Philo, Josephus, and a great multitude of others, whose genuineness no one seriously questions. Nay, we have even genuine Christian writings of that same period in which our New Testament according to the critics originated. The genuineness of these heathen, Jewish, and even Christian, writings is conceded, although it is not better attested than that of the Pauline Epistles. Is not this an inconsistency? By no means. There was for the most part no urgent motive for putting out books in the name of the great men of the heathen world. This was done more or less, it is true, by those who wished thus to secure attention to their productions. But the sacred cause of the Christian religion demanded efficient measures; and inasmuch as the Church a century after Christ's time found itself without any canonical apostolical writings, and there was imminent danger that the Church would be split up into numberless contending parties and go to pieces irretrievably, there was an imperative necessity of somehow averting this danger. And this could be accomplished only by means of pseudepigraphy.

One more question may possibly be asked: Why should it have been the case that in the heathen world men of note produced noted writings, whereas in the early Christian Church the leading men wrote nothing, and the influential and really able writings of that period were written by unknown and apparently mediocre persons? Is it not intrinsically improbable that there should have been this difference? Well, we are under no obligations to answer such questions. Our business is to find out the facts, not to make every fact seem natural and intelligible to every body. Still we may attempt to give a reason why it is really for the best that the authors of the Bible should be entirely unknown. True, men naturally like to know something about the authors of their favourite books. They are prone to ascribe great books to great men. But this is after all a childish weakness. The value of what is written does not depend on the writer, but is something intrinsic. That which is true and instructive is true and instructive, whether we know anything about the author or not. Strictly speaking, it is better not to know anything about him. For if we think of the person, we are likely to be influenced more or less by the real or supposed character of the author instead of by what he says. It is, therefore, to be regarded as the arrangement of a beneficent Providence that perfect obscurity conceals the origin of our Biblical books, so that we are not tempted to forget the great truths in our glorification of those who have uttered them.

It is of course not romantic to be obliged to talk about the writings of J, E, P, JE, G, JC, etc., instead of about the writings of Moses, David, John, or Paul. But, properly considered, this will be found to be the very excellence, and even sublimity, of the result of criticism, that personality is put out of sight, that personal peculiarities can have no weight in our judgment of published works. As in algebra great truths are best expressed when the quantities are designated by letters insignificant in themselves, so in the sphere of religion we have attained the highest point when we know nothing about the persons who first uttered great thoughts or produced immortal writings. Accordingly it would really be well if all writings were anonymous or pseudonymous, if all orators could speak unseen, or rather (since even the audible voice often exercises a biasing effect) if there were no orators at all, and every thing thought and expressed could be found only in the unimpassioned form of anonymous writings. Then every one would be able to judge all subjects impartially; and beyond a doubt the world would soon begin to agree on the vexed questions which now agitate it. It should, therefore, be a source of rejoicing, when the critic expunges from the most distinguished productions all traces of personal relations and characteristics. When this is fully accomplished, the naked thought, the simple truth, towers aloft, like a great pyramid whose sublime form one can view and admire without being distracted by any thought of the king or the architect who first conceived or executed the work.

POSTSCRIPT.

A brief history of the foregoing treatise may fittingly be given here. Some time ago I conceived the plan of undertaking, as a *jeu d'esprit*, to prove the Epistle to the Romans to be a compilation of various non-Pauline elements. When I began, I knew that besides Bruno Bauer's almost forgotten effort, one or two Dutch critics had questioned the genuineness of the Epistle. But I had not seen their works, and I assumed the Pauline authorship of the Epistle to be so generally admitted and so incontrovertible that the very fact of my pretending to dispute it would betray the irony of the effort. When I had drawn out the argument in its main features, I heard of Steck's work; and when my essay was finished, that of Völter appeared; so that, mine being published after theirs, it could not be expected to be so self-evident that it is a travesty as I had at first assumed. Still the main object which I had in mind is not nullified by these works; they only make it the more needful that it should here be plainly stated what the real intent of my treatise is. I may add that, while I believe fully in the Pauline authorship of the Epistle to the Romans, I still think that l have made out a stronger case for the spuriousness and composite character of the Epistle than the real doubters themselves have done. And by the exercise of sufficient ingenuity equally plausible efforts might unquestionably be made with many other ancient and even modern works, about whose genuineness there is not the slightest doubt in any well-balanced mind. The reader will draw his own moral.

E. D. M^c R.

T. and T. Clark's Publications.

In demy 8vo, price 10s. 6d.,

THE JEWISH
AND
THE CHRISTIAN MESSIAH.

A STUDY IN THE EARLIEST HISTORY OF CHRISTIANITY.

By Professor VINCENT HENRY STANTON, M.A.,
TRINITY COLLEGE, CAMBRIDGE.

'Mr. Stanton's book answers a real want, and will be indispensable to students of the origin of Christianity. We hope that Mr. Stanton will be able to continue his labours in that most obscure and most important period, of his competency to deal with which he has given such good proof in this book.'—*Guardian.*

'We welcome this book as a valuable addition to the literature of a most important subject. . . . The book is remarkable for the clearness of its style. Mr. Stanton is never obscure from beginning to end, and we think that no reader of average attainments will be able to put the book down without having learnt much from his lucid and scholarly exposition.'—*Ecclesiastical Gazette.*

Now complete, in Five Volumes, 8vo, price 10s. 6d. each,

HISTORY OF THE JEWISH PEOPLE IN THE TIME OF OUR LORD.

By Dr. EMIL SCHÜRER,
PROFESSOR OF THEOLOGY IN THE UNIVERSITY OF KIEL.

TRANSLATED FROM THE SECOND EDITION (REVISED THROUGHOUT, AND GREATLY ENLARGED) OF '*HISTORY OF THE NEW TESTAMENT TIMES.*'

*** Professor Schürer has prepared an exhaustive INDEX to this work, to which he attaches great value. The Translation is now ready, and is issued in a separate Volume (100 pp. 8vo). Price 2s. 6d. *nett*.

'Under Professor Schürer's guidance we are enabled to a large extent to construct a social and political framework for the Gospel History, and to set it in such a light as to see new evidences of the truthfulness of that history and of its contemporaneousness. . . . The length of our notice shows our estimate of the value of his work.'—*English Churchman.*

'Messrs. Clark have afresh earned the thanks of all students of the New Testament in England, by undertaking to present Schürer's masterly work in a form easily accessible to the English reader. . . . In every case the amount of research displayed is very great, truly German in its proportions, while the style of Professor Schürer is by no means cumbrous, after the manner of some of his countrymen. We have inadequately described a most valuable work, but we hope we have said enough to induce our readers who do not know this book to seek it out forthwith.'—*Methodist Recorder.*

*

T. and T. Clark's Publications.

GRIMM'S LEXICON.

'The best New Testament Greek Lexicon. . . . It is a treasury of the results of exact scholarship.'—BISHOP WESTCOTT.

In demy 4to, Third Edition, price 36s.,

A GREEK-ENGLISH LEXICON OF THE NEW TESTAMENT,

BEING

GRIMM'S 'WILKE'S CLAVIS NOVI TESTAMENTI.'

Translated, Revised, and Enlarged

BY

JOSEPH HENRY THAYER, D.D.,

BUSSEY PROFESSOR OF NEW TESTAMENT CRITICISM AND INTERPRETATION IN THE DIVINITY SCHOOL OF HARVARD UNIVERSITY.

EXTRACT FROM PREFACE.

'TOWARDS the close of the year 1862, the "Arnoldische Buchhandlung" in Leipzig published the First Part of a Greek-Latin Lexicon of the New Testament, prepared upon the basis of the "Clavis Novi Testamenti Philologica" of C. G. Wilke (second edition, 2 vols. 1851), by Professor C. L. WILIBALD GRIMM of Jena. In his Prospectus, Professor Grimm announced it as his purpose not only (in accordance with the improvements in classical lexicography embodied in the Paris edition of Stephen's Thesaurus and in the fifth edition of Passow's Dictionary edited by Rost and his coadjutors) to exhibit the historical growth of a word's significations, and accordingly in selecting his vouchers for New Testament usage to show at what time and in what class of writers a given word became current, but also duly to notice the usage of the Septuagint and of the Old Testament Apocrypha, and especially to produce a Lexicon which should correspond to the present condition of textual criticism, of exegesis, and of biblical theology. He devoted more than seven years to his task. The successive Parts of his work received, as they appeared, the outspoken commendation of scholars diverging as widely in their views as Hupfeld and Hengstenberg; and since its completion in 1868 it has been generally acknowledged to be by far the best Lexicon of the New Testament extant.'

'The best New Testament Greek Lexicon. . . . It is a treasury of the results of exact scholarship.'—BISHOP WESTCOTT.

'I regard it as a work of the greatest importance. . . . It seems to me a work showing the most patient diligence, and the most carefully arranged collection of useful and helpful references.'—THE BISHOP OF GLOUCESTER AND BRISTOL.

'The use of Professor Grimm's book for years has convinced me that it is not only unquestionably the best among existing New Testament Lexicons, but that, apart from all comparisons, it is a work of the highest intrinsic merit, and one which is admirably adapted to initiate a learner into an acquaintance with the language of the New Testament. It ought to be regarded as one of the first and most necessary requisites for the study of the New Testament, and consequently for the study of theology in general.'—Professor EMIL SCHÜRER.

T. and T. Clark's Publications.

HERZOG'S BIBLICAL ENCYCLOPÆDIA.

Now complete, in Three Vols. imp. 8vo, price 24s. each,

ENCYCLOPÆDIA OR DICTIONARY

OF

Biblical, Historical, Doctrinal, and Practical Theology.

Based on the Real-Encyclopädie of Herzog, Plitt, and Hauck.

EDITED BY PHILIP SCHAFF, D.D., LL.D.

'A well-designed, meritorious work, on which neither industry nor expense has been spared.'—*Guardian.*

'This certainly is a remarkable work. . . . It will be one without which no general or theological or biographical library will be complete.'—*Freeman.*

'The need of such a work as this must be very often felt, and it ought to find its way into all college libraries, and into many private studies.'—*Christian World.*

'As a comprehensive work of reference, within a moderate compass, we know nothing at all equal to it in the large department which it deals with.'—*Church Bells.*

SUPPLEMENT TO HERZOG'S ENCYCLOPÆDIA.

In Imperial 8vo, price 8s.,

ENCYCLOPÆDIA OF LIVING DIVINES.

'A very useful Encyclopædia. I am very glad to have it for frequent reference.'—Right Rev. BISHOP LIGHTFOOT.

Now complete, in Four Vols. imp. 8vo, price 12s. 6d. each,

COMMENTARY ON THE NEW TESTAMENT.

With Illustrations and Maps.

EDITED BY PHILIP SCHAFF, D.D., LL.D.

Volume I.	*Volume II.*
THE SYNOPTICAL GOSPELS.	**ST. JOHN'S GOSPEL** AND THE **ACTS OF THE APOSTLES.**
Volume III.	*Volume IV.*
ROMANS to PHILEMON.	**HEBREWS to REVELATION.**

'A useful, valuable, and instructive commentary. The interpretation is set forth with clearness and cogency, and in a manner calculated to commend the volumes to the thoughtful reader. The book is beautifully got up, and reflects great credit on the publishers as well as the writers.'—THE BISHOP OF GLOUCESTER.

'There are few better commentaries having a similar scope and object; indeed, within the same limits, we do not know of one so good, upon the whole, of the New Testament.'—*Literary World.*

'External beauty and intrinsic worth combine in the work here completed. Good paper, good type, good illustrations, good binding please the eye, as accuracy and thoroughness in matter of treatment satisfy the judgment. Everywhere the workmanship is careful, solid, harmonious.'—*Methodist Recorder.*

T. and T. Clark's Publications.

LOTZE'S MICROCOSMUS.

In Two Vols. 8vo, FOURTH EDITION, price 36s.,

MICROCOSMUS:
CONCERNING MAN AND HIS RELATION TO THE WORLD.
By HERMANN LOTZE.

CONTENTS:— Book I. The Body. II. The Soul. III. Life. IV. Man. V. Mind. VI. The Microcosmic Order; or, The Course of Human Life. VII. History. VIII. Progress. IX. The Unity of Things.

'These are indeed two masterly volumes, vigorous in intellectual power, and translated with rare ability. . . . This work will doubtless find a place on the shelves of all the foremost thinkers and students of modern times.'— *Evangelical Magazine.*

'The English public have now before them the greatest philosophic work produced in Germany by the generation just past. The translation comes at an opportune time, for the circumstances of English thought, just at the present moment, are peculiarly those with which Lotze attempted to deal when he wrote his "Microcosmus," a quarter of a century ago. . . . Few philosophic books of the century are so attractive both in style and matter.'— *Athenæum.*

'Lotze is the ablest, the most brilliant, and most renowned of the German philosophers of to-day. . . . He has rendered invaluable and splendid service to Christian thinkers, and has given them a work which cannot fail to equip them for the sturdiest intellectual conflicts and to ensure their victory.'— *Baptist Magazine.*

In Two Vols. 8vo, price 21s.,

NATURE AND THE BIBLE:
LECTURES ON THE MOSAIC HISTORY OF CREATION IN ITS RELATION TO NATURAL SCIENCE.

By DR. FR. H. REUSCH.

REVISED AND CORRECTED BY THE AUTHOR.

Translated from the Fourth Edition
By KATHLEEN LYTTELTON.

'Other champions much more competent and learned than myself might have been placed in the field; I will only name one of the most recent, Dr. Reusch, author of "Nature and the Bible."'—The Right Hon. W. E. GLADSTONE.

'The work, we need hardly say, is of profound and perennial interest, and it can scarcely be too highly commended as, in many respects, a very successful attempt to settle one of the most perplexing questions of the day. It is impossible to read it without obtaining larger views of theology, and more accurate opinions respecting its relations to science, and no one will rise from its perusal without feeling a deep sense of gratitude to its author.'—*Scottish Review.*

www.ingramcontent.com/pod-product-compliance
Lightning Source LLC
Chambersburg PA
CBHW020151170426
43199CB00010B/987